Praise for The Veg-Feasting Cookbook

"A good cookbook is like a trusted guide when entering new territory. Without the guide there may be reticence and even failure to go forward. With a trusted guide, progress is made into new areas with confidence and pleasure.

From a doctor's standpoint, I am pleased to endorse a vegetarian cookbook—particularly this cookbook—because I know the power of phytochemicals in vegetarian food to decrease the pain of arthritis, lessen the danger of the common degenerative diseases such as cancer, heart disease and diabetes. And all of these wonderful advantages are experienced, along with the pleasure of eating really good food, at no extra cost of pills or expensive potions!

Why should I say more? Just enjoy vegetarian food and feel better, think clearer and faster, and live longer while feeling great! You can only prove it one way—try it!"

—*Ray Foster, M.D.*

"Healthy international vegetarian meals to suit every taste. Here you can find wonderful vegan recipes for snacks, a meal or a party. For added measure, you'll get the latest information on the Pacific Northwest vegetarian scene."

—*Susan Gins, M.S. Nutrition, Bastyr University, Certified Nutritionist*

"A lowfat vegetarian diet rich in fruits, vegetables and whole grains has powerfully health-promoting effects. I wish you these positive physical, mental and emotional effects as you eat for health."

—*Gregory Scribner, M.D.*

The Veg-Feasting Cookbook

Favorite recipes from local restaurants and leading chefs in the Pacific Northwest

By Vegetarians of Washington

Book Publishing Company
Summertown, Tennessee

Editors: Amanda Strombom

                      Stewart Rose

Managing Editor: Griggs Irving

Food Editor: Cheryl Redmond

Cover Design: Warren Jefferson

Interior Design: Edwina Cusolito

Cover Photos: © PhotoDisk, Inc.

Book Publishing Company
P.O. Box 99
Summertown, TN 38483
1-888-260-8458
bookpubco.com

Printed in Canada by Transcontinental.

ISBN 1-57067-178-8

10 09 08 07 06 05 1 2 3 4 5 6 7 8 9

The material in this book is not a substitute for professional medical care. Please consult your physician before making any changes to your diet, lifestyle or medications.

The Book Publishing Co. is committed to preserving ancient forests and natural resources. We have elected to print this title on Williamsburg Recycled, which is 30% postconsumer recycled and processed chlorine free. As a result of our paper choice, we have saved the following natural resources:

29 trees (40 feet in height)
1,349 lbs. of solid waste
12,234 gallons of water
4,920 kwh of electricity
2,649 pounds of greenhouse gases

BOOK
PUBLISHING
COMPANY

We are a member of Green Press Initiative. For more information about Green Press Initiative visit: www.greenpressinitiative.org

Library of Congress Cataloging-in-Publication Data

The Veg-Feasting Cookbook: favorite recipes from local restaurants and leading chefs in the Pacific Northwest /
by Vegetarians of Washington.
    p. cm.
  Includes index.
  ISBN 1-57067-178-8
  1. Vegetarian cookery. 2. Cookery—Northwest, Pacific.
  I. Vegetarians of Washington.
TX837.V416 2005
641.5'636'09795—dc22
                        2004030404

Contents

Recipes

Acknowledgements

We thank the farmers, manufacturers, distributors, brokers, retailers and restaurateurs who form the vital links in our food chain. We would especially like to thank all the restaurants, delis, chefs, cookbook authors and others who so generously supported the creation of this book with their recipes.

We greatly appreciate the assistance of our food editor Cheryl Redmond and book designer Edwina Cusolito. Without their professional support and services we could not have produced this cookbook.

We feel very fortunate to have the Book Publishing Company as the publisher of this book. Special thanks go to Bob and Cynthia Holzapfel and all the other folks at the Book Publishing Company who have done so much to help make this book a success.

We are very grateful for help and encouragement from Charles Stahler and the whole team at the Vegetarian Resource Group.

We would like to thank Casey Blake, Shaleen Gilson, Casey MacDonald and Jessica Dadds for their work on this project. Thanks also to Celia and Peter Heathcote for their continued support and the many other volunteers and supporters of this project too numerous to mention.

Our ultimate thanks go to all the volunteers and members of Vegetarians of Washington for their support of the organization and its mission.

Amanda Strombom, *President*
Stewart Rose, *Vice President*
Griggs Irving, *Managing Editor*
Vegetarians of Washington

Introduction

The Veg-Feasting Cookbook offers you culinary delights from the many different kinds of vegetarian cuisine represented in the Pacific Northwest. Many of the best restaurants in Washington and Oregon have shared their culinary secrets by offering us some of their most popular recipes. In addition, we've included recipes from some of the country's best cookbook authors and chefs who were chosen to be featured at Vegfest, the annual vegetarian food festival held in the Seattle Center each year. The result is a unique cookbook, with recipes not easily obtainable elsewhere.

The Veg-Feasting Cookbook is organized into convenient chapters, with recipes for breakfast, appetizers, soups, salads and dressings, entrees and desserts. With recipes reflecting the wide range of cuisine found in the many vegetarian and veg-friendly restaurants throughout the Northwest, you'll feel like you're on a world tour as you try one tempting recipe after the other.

These delicious recipes vary from the elegantly simple to the simply gourmet, with many recipes using special ingredients. As you travel through the recipes you'll find special ingredients are either described in a box on the same page, or cross referenced to another part of the book so that you can learn about the ingredients in more detail.

The Veg-Feasting Cookbook is much more than just a compilation of recipes. You'll also learn all about the exciting veg scene in the Pacific Northwest, the many benefits of a vegetarian diet, and how to put together a balanced diet based on the four new food groups. There is a detailed guide to the full range of ingredients used in vegetarian cooking, with suggestions on how to buy and cook with many different varieties of herbs and spices.

After the success of our popular travel guidebook, *Veg-Feasting in the Pacific Northwest*, we received many requests for recipes from the restaurants and delis featured in that book. We are happy we can now meet these requests. With this new cookbook, you can enjoy food usually only available in the Northwest's best restaurants, right in your own home.

Whether at home or out on the town, Vegetarians of Washington is here to guide you through one delicious meal after the other…Enjoy!

A Wise and Delicious Choice

By Stewart Rose
Vice President
Vegetarians of Washington

Food is there to be enjoyed! There's no doubt about it. However, many people feel that they're caught in a bind. They want to enjoy delicious food, but at the same time they worry that the food they most enjoy is the least healthy for them. Many people also feel that the idea of consuming animals for food weighs heavily on their minds, but resign themselves to eating meat, thinking that it's us or them. When people discover how environmentally unsound animal agriculture is, they often say "But I have to eat to live!"

In light of all this, Vegetarians of Washington would like to offer you this deal. You can enjoy the most delicious food you can imagine, and at the same time greatly improve your health, while easing your conscience about the animals and the environment. Sound good? We think so too, so we wrote this cookbook to help more people to get in on a good deal.

Let's talk about enjoying our food first. We admit it, we love great tasting food and we'll accept nothing less. The fact is that vegetarian food has come in to its own as the most desirable of cuisines, attracting the world's most noted chefs and cookbook authors. The restaurants in the Northwest have caught on and we've included recipes from the region's best restaurants and natural food market delis. We'll help you learn the secrets of delicious food. In this book you'll find lots of information on how to get started. Look for shopping and cooking tips on healthy food and lots of information on ingredients that may be new to you throughout the book. We'll grab you by the taste buds and we won't let go!

The land, the air and the water are so much a part of our lives. There's a good feeling that comes from helping to sustain the environment. While some people think of helping the environment by recycling, we think of enjoying a veggieburger! The satisfaction of eating in a way that protects the environment makes the food taste even better.

Today's factory raised animals have a much rougher time than they used to. The animals are our friends, so let's give Elsie the Cow a well deserved vacation. While good old Elsie is enjoying her vacation, we can also enjoy ours in excellent health. It's another win-win situation.

Trying new foods and learning as you go will give you a chance to be creative. The secrets of success on your journey are to be willing to experiment with new foods, to be willing to learn, to proceed at your own pace and to just do the best you can. We take the optimistic approach. However far you come on your journey makes you that much further ahead.

Just who are those vegetarians anyway? The big news is that vegetarians are everywhere these days and, in fact, they have always been an important part of our society. They have made contributions in all walks of life throughout history. Examples include Albert Einstein in science; Thomas Edison in industry; baseball and football stars in sports such as Hank Aaron, the homerun king, and Desmond Howard, the Superbowl MVP; Paul McCartney of the Beatles; and founding fathers such as Benjamin Franklin. But most vegetarians are not famous. They're the people who live next door, the lady who sits next to you at work or the guy standing behind you in line at the movies. They're everyday people.

Vegetarians of Washington was founded by everyday people. We welcome everyone whether you're a vegetarian, a beginner or just curious. We're having a good time discovering new and tasty foods, and we invite you to join in the adventure and the fun.

The Vegetarian Scene in the Pacific Northwest

By Stewart Rose
Vice President
Vegetarians of Washington

The vegetarian scene in the Northwest provides a delicious diversity as well as a fascinating history. Several segments of the community have combined over time to form a unique Northwest flavor that continues to nourish the growing vegetarian scene to this day. The local recipe combines elements of the health food folks, people working for animal welfare, a new breed of environmentalists and many people of faith.

How is it that these diverse groups found common ground in a vegetarian diet? And how did it lead to the Pacific Northwest having the most dynamic and exciting veg-scene in the country? To answer these questions we must turn the clock all the way back to the 1700s.

Benjamin Franklin was one of America's first vegetarians and also is credited with introducing the soybean to the United States. Who thought then that Ben Franklin's humble soybean would some day be found in the Northwest's most posh restaurants and trendiest natural food stores? The late 1800s brought some drastic changes in the American diet. Under the mistaken notion that heavily refined food and lots of meat represented progress and prosperity, the national diet changed to include more of these foods. Enter white bread and refined sugar, and spoiled and decaying meat so bad that it sparked national scandals made famous by Upton Sinclair in *The Jungle*. Enter also an increase in diseases such as heart disease, cancer, diabetes and several digestive disorders. Many people looked at the changes in our diet and health and wondered if it wasn't time to return to a healthier, more traditional diet.

About this time, one group in particular advocated a return to a healthier diet. It advocated a return all the way back to Adam and Eve. That group was the Seventh Day Adventists, a new church especially popular in the Northwest. This group worked to improve the diet and health of every man, woman and child in the Northwest and throughout the country, by actively promoting a healthy vegetarian diet and by founding new health food companies. These companies also manufactured some of the early meat substitutes that have recently become so popular. The ones they sell these days are so real my cat starts to meow when I open them!

By the early 1900s some other church groups began recommending a vegetarian diet. For example, the Unity Christian church and the Salvation Army started to promote a vegetarian diet at about this time. Soon, many other religious groups were also starting to take a closer look at a vegetarian diet. The vegetarian movement in the Northwest and in the rest of the country was now gaining momentum.

By the time the Roaring Twenties (1920s) arrived, modern medicine was coming into its own with major advances in medicine and surgery to benefit both young and old. But doctors also began noticing an increase in the incidence of those diseases they suspected were linked to the national changes in diet. They noticed that vegetarians were usually the healthiest folks in town. The day would come when everyone from country doctors to the Surgeon General would tout the benefits of a vegetarian diet. Health conscious people across the Northwest would start saying "please pass the tofu" and natural food markets would spring up across the region to meet the demand.

As the country grew so did the need for large quantities of inexpensive food. Old MacDonald's farm was a thing of the past. Enter the factory farm and really hard times for the animals. Animal Welfare groups emerged all over the country, including the Northwest. These folks, motivated by humanitarian considerations, became some of the most enthusiastic proponents of a vegetarian diet, saving the animals with every bite.

Along with the many innovations of the 1960s came a new and vital influence in the vegetarian movement. The call was to get back to a more natural way of life. Many more began turning to a vegetarian diet. Many were also getting down to business as the Northwest became home to a number of vegetarian food companies founded with a vegetarian vision. Soon, natural food co-ops and vegetarian restaurants began springing up all over the Northwest. Bulk bins for grains, beans sold by the pound, and scrambled tofu for breakfast were becoming more common. Yoga also was becoming popular in the Northwest with many Yoga instructors advocating a vegetarian diet to their students.

During the 1970s and '80s the environmental movement came into its own. We heard about the Amazon and other rainforests being cut and burned down primarily to raise meat. The oil shortages of the '70s made us more conscious of just how much more oil was needed to produce meat compared to vegetarian foods. We smelled the runoff from factory farms into our streams. Many environmentalists realized that following a vegetarian diet is a way to help preserve the environment for future generations.

The 1980s and '90s brought quite a bit of immigration to the Northwest with a substantial number of new people coming from Asia. Many of these people were Buddhists from China, Thailand and Vietnam who brought a tradition of vegetarianism with them. Others came from India where following a vegetarian diet is an age-old Hindu tradition. The new wave of immigration led to a new wave of vegetarian restaurants featuring a rich variety of ethnic cuisine. A new health-conscious trend among some Mexican restaurants offered new menu items such as vegan burritos. The choice of vegetarian cuisine in the Northwest was growing quickly.

From fine dining in Seattle and Portland's vegetarian restaurants and bistros, to great home cooking in Washington and Oregon's small town cafés and eateries, the Northwest now offers culinary delights to satisfy every taste and desire.

Not to be overlooked is the monthly dining event of the Vegetarians of Washington. This culinary happening features a different restaurant, cookbook author or chef every month at a downtown Seattle location that draws people from near and far.

There's also Vegfest, the country's largest and most exciting vegetarian food festival. Vegfest features chefs from all over the country who show their magic and share their secrets in large-scale cooking demonstrations. Doctors and dietitians are on hand to talk about the latest health advantages of a vegetarian diet. Vegfest also features the largest vegetarian bookstore in the world. Here in the Northwest, we love to try new food. Vegfest satisfies this desire by featuring more than 400 different kinds of food to taste. Each year, this food sampling extravaganza serves the vegetarian and veg-curious public with more than 150,000 free samples of delicious food from every company you've ever heard of and a few you haven't, but soon will.

Following a vegetarian diet never has been more popular and has started to go mainstream. Vegetarian food is all the rage here and we invite you to try the recipes in this book and discover the delicious vegetarian cuisine to be found in the Pacific Northwest.

The Four New Food Groups

By Amanda Strombom
President
Vegetarians of Washington

Everyone, from Nobel Prize winning doctors to Surgeons General, is recommending a vegetarian diet these days. One report after the other shows that vegetarians live longer and have much lower rates of heart disease, cancer, diabetes and many other diseases. But just how do they do it? Do they walk through the market with charts and calculators following some complicated formula? What's their secret?

Well, it's no secret and it's as easy as can be. Vegetarians simply include food from each of the Four New Groups every day in their diet. The Four New Food Groups are Legumes, Whole Grains, Fruits and Vegetables. By choosing a variety of food from these four food groups, vegetarians follow a diet that has made them the healthiest people in town. And the best part of it all is that vegetarian food is so delicious!

Just what's included in each of the Four New Food Groups?

Legumes

Legumes include peas, lentils and all kinds of beans—soybeans, chickpeas, kidney beans, black beans, white beans, even peanuts. All are packed with protein, complex carbohydrates including lots of fiber, calcium, iron and even have some essential fatty acids. They have no cholesterol and make a great replacement for meat in your diet. Lentils, black beans and garbanzo beans are especially digestible. Try lentils in a Shepherd's Pie (page 150), black beans in a soup (page 68) or salad (page 85), and garbanzo beans in Hummus (page 51) or an Indian curry (page 177) for example.

Don't forget the many soy products which are available. Recent medical studies have confirmed the benefits of soy. Tofu and tempeh offer particularly versatile ways to include soy in your diet. See the index for many different ways to prepare these products in delicious recipes. Many of today's meat-substitute products are based on soy too, including veggie burgers, meatless hot dogs, soy jerky, fake bacon, pepperoni and bologna. Dairy substitutes such as soy milk, soy "cheese," soy "yogurt" and soy "ice cream" have also become very popular. These should all be available at your local natural food store.

Although technically not legumes, nuts and seeds also are high in protein and provide an excellent source of vitamins, minerals, essential fatty acids and fiber. Include a handful of walnuts, cashews, almonds, brazil nuts or hazelnuts in your diet several times a week, or try nut butters for spreads, dips and sauces. Seeds like pumpkin seeds, sesame seeds and sunflower seeds add nutrients and crunch to your diet. Tahini, sesame seed butter, is one of the key ingredients in hummus which is a great dip for vegetables.

Whole Grains

Whole Grains include wheat, oats, barley, buckwheat, brown rice, cereals, pasta and whole grain breads of every kind. Also included are alternate grains, such as quinoa and amaranth, which are finding their way into many recipes and quickly increasing in popularity. Whole grains are powerhouses of energy and nutrition with generous amounts of protein, vitamins such as the B vitamins and vitamin E, minerals such as iron and zinc, and fiber. There's an endless variety of ways to include whole grains in your diet. Try whole wheat toast or oatmeal for breakfast, a whole grain burrito or pasta for lunch and rice or quinoa with your supper. Everyone needs some treats once in a while, so use whole grain flour and natural sweeteners, with cocoa or dark chocolate chips if you like, to make tasty cakes and cookies for a treat. See the Desserts section for many delicious healthy recipes.

Vegetables

The range of vegetables available is amazing, and every one of them is packed with vitamins, minerals and fiber. Choose from among the cruciferous vegetables: broccoli, cauliflower, Brussels sprouts, cabbage, kale and collard greens. These vegetables are especially well regarded both for their nutritional content and for their protective value against several diseases. Green leafy vegetables such as chard, spinach, arugula and the many varieties of lettuce provide excellent nutrition in salads. Tomatoes and peppers (technically fruits) of all varieties are great for salads and sauces and are high in vitamins and antioxidants. Eggplants and potatoes make great foundations for any meal. Versatile vegetables can be served as a salad, a side dish or a main dish and can be steamed, baked or stir fried.

Fruits

There's an abundance of fruits to choose from. Examples of berries include blackberries, blueberries, strawberries, raspberries and cranberries. Citrus fruits include oranges, tangerines, lemons and grapefruit. Melons include cantaloupe, honeydew and watermelon. Tree and vine fruits include apples, peaches, bananas, figs and grapes. Tropical fruit include mangoes, papayas and kiwis. All fruits are loaded with vitamins, especially vitamin C. There's a lot of evidence that fruits help reduce the risk of certain diseases, so choose a variety of fresh fruits to eat every day. They make ideal snacks and desserts and are scrumptious additions to salads.

Putting it all together

Combine choices from these four food groups, add a few herbs, spices and other natural flavorings (oils, vinegars or sweeteners as needed) and you have everything you need for delicious and healthy meals. Look through the index. This book has many recipes which will help you incorporate these ingredients.

In addition to food, doctors recommend drinking 6 to 8 cups of water every day, as an essential component to your diet. Taking a daily multivitamin helps make sure you are getting all you need and supplies vitamin B_{12}, which is needed for diets which include no animal products.

Our guidebook *Veg-Feasting in the Pacific Northwest* contains much more information on nutrition and the many advantages of a vegetarian diet, written by doctors and dietitians. There you'll find in-depth articles on feeding babies and their mothers, and attracting children to healthier foods. There are also special sections for athletes, women and seniors. You will also find more information how a vegetarian diet helps prevent diseases such as heart attacks, strokes, cancer, osteoporosis and diabetes. For more information about this book, see page 239.

For more important information on how to buy, store and cook the foods in the new four food groups, see the Vegetarian Kitchen article on page 19.

The Vegetarian Kitchen

By Cheryl Redmond
Food Editor

Preparing meals that are both delicious and healthful is easy if you have the right ingredients on hand. Choose foods that give you a lot of bang for your culinary buck, foods that offer great flavor, great nutrition, and if possible, convenience too. Take extra-virgin olive oil, for instance. It's high in monounsaturated fats, which are good for your heart, and its spicy, fruity flavor complements salads, grains and dozens of other dishes. Or quinoa, an ancient grain with an appealing, lightly crunchy texture that's extremely high in protein and is quick and easy to cook. Read on for more ingredients that deserve a place in your healthy kitchen.

LEGUMES

Beans and Lentils
Beans are tiny bundles of energy, providing complex carbohydrates, protein, soluble fiber, calcium, B vitamins and folate. Dried beans are the most economical and aren't difficult to cook; they just require a little planning ahead. When buying dried beans, shop at a store with a high turnover and look for beans that are plump and smooth, not shriveled. Canned beans make a quicker, more convenient alternative and will work fine in most recipes that call for dried. Often, organic brands are lower in sodium than conventional brands. Here are some common bean varieties:

Adzuki (also spelled azuki or aduki) beans, are small dark reddish brown beans with a mild sweet flavor, used in Japanese cooking.

Black beans, or turtle beans, are used in Latin American and Caribbean cooking, and go particularly well with spicy foods and citrus flavors.

Black-eyed peas, or cowpeas are popular in Southern cuisine. They contribute their mild, earthy flavor to the dish called Hoppin' John.

Chickpeas, or garbanzo beans, are used in Mediterranean cooking. Firm and nutty, they're great in soups, salads, and indispensable for hummus.

Kidney beans are robust and meaty, and can hold their own in dishes like red beans and rice. A type of French kidney bean, called the flageolet, has a delicate celadon color and is mild and tender.

Lima beans, or butter beans, are large, pale green beans, most famously paired with corn to make succotash.

Pinto beans, with their pink and brown markings and hearty flavor, are used in refried beans. They work well in chili and other stews.

Great Northern beans, navy beans (also called Yankee beans), and **cannellini** are all mild-tasting white beans, good in soups. Large great Northern beans and small navy beans are both used for baked beans.

Lentils are the exception to the canned-beans-are-fine rule; canned lentils tend to be mushy. Fortunately, dried lentils cook quickly and don't need to be pre-soaked, making them suitable for weeknight dinners. Varieties include common brown lentils, also known as green lentils; French green lentils, also called lentilles de Puy; beluga lentils which are small and black; and red lentils, which cook quickly, becoming soft and golden. Green and beluga lentils are suited for soups or salads; red lentils are best in soups.

Dal is the Indian name for peas, beans and lentils that have been split and sometimes skinned; they're sold in Indian markets. Varieties include chana dal (from a relative of the chickpea), masoor dal (from pink lentils), moong dal (from mung beans), toor dal (from yellow lentils), and urid dal (from black lentils, although the dal is white because the lentils have been skinned).

Soyfoods

Soyfoods are valued not only for their protein (they contain all the essential amino acids) but for their cancer-fighting isoflavones. You can find myriad soy-containing products on the market, some very highly processed. But for the greatest health benefit and versatility in the kitchen, choose traditional, minimally processed soyfoods.

Edamame are green soybeans. You can buy them fresh or frozen, in the pod or out. In their pods, they make a wonderful snack or appetizer, steamed and sprinkled with coarse salt. Use your teeth to pull the beans from their pods. Shelled edamame are a tasty addition to soups and stand in for lima beans in dishes like succotash. Edamame are fun to grow; if you have a garden, consider planting a row or two of these protein-filled legumes.

Miso has a savory quality (called umami in Japan) that provides depth of flavor to soups, sauces and dressings. It's also a rich source of the isoflavones genistein and daidzen, believed to have a protective effect against cancer. Miso is primarily made of soy, but may include barley, chickpeas or rice. The color and flavor of miso depend on its ingredients and fermentation time. Generally speaking, dark misos have been aged longer and have a more assertive, saltier taste than lighter ones. All miso is very salty, so add a little at a time, tasting as you go. Unpasteurized miso, sold in the refrigerated case, contains beneficial enzymes that aid digestion. If you're using unpasteurized miso in soups or stews, add it at the end of cooking to preserve its healthful qualities.

Tempeh has a chewy texture and a hearty, somewhat mushroom-like flavor. It's well worthwhile making friends with this nutritional superstar. One serving packs 20 grams of protein, 6 grams of fiber, and plenty of cancer-fighting soy isoflavones. And it's low in fat.

Tempeh is made from soybeans that have been cooked and fermented with a special culture that binds the beans together into a firm, sliceable patty. The fermentation process also makes tempeh easy to digest. Tempeh easily absorbs flavors and can be baked, boiled, fried or steamed.

Tofu's smooth texture and mild flavor make it a kitchen chameleon, able to transform itself into main dishes as well as desserts. Most tofu is enriched with calcium chloride, so it's a good source of calcium as well as protein. There are two basic types; regular (momen) and silken (kinugoshi). Regular tofu may be labeled soft, firm or extra firm, with softer tofu more suitable for blending and firmer more suitable for frying. Silken tofu is most suitable for desserts and smoothies where a creamy texture is required. Firmness varies from brand to brand, however, so you may need to experiment. You can also buy low-fat, preflavored, baked or smoked tofu. Tofu is available in refrigerated or aseptic packaging, and in bulk. Whatever kind you buy, once you open the package, cover any unused tofu with water and refrigerate it until needed.

Soymilk comes in a variety of flavors, but to replace cow's milk in recipes like quiche or mashed potatoes, stick to the plain, unsweetened kind. Most brands of soymilk are enriched with calcium and other nutrients, and have a protein content similar to milk. Like milk, soymilk will curdle; adding 1 tablespoon of lemon juice or vinegar to a cup of soymilk will make a buttermilk substitute. And like milk, soymilk can spoil; keep refrigerated cartons and opened aseptic cartons cold, and use open cartons within a week.

Soy sauce is a brew of fermented soybeans and roasted wheat, with water and salt added. It can range from light and thin (not to be confused with low-sodium) to dark and thick. Thai thin soy sauce is an example of the former style, while Chinese black sweet soy sauce is an example of the latter. Shoyu is the Japanese word for soy sauce. Tamari is Japanese soy sauce that has been brewed without wheat. It is slightly thicker and richer tasting than regular soy sauce. The best soy sauce is aged and contains no additives. Soy sauce is salty; one tablespoon provides more than a third of your daily value for sodium, so use it sparingly. "Lite" or low-sodium soy sauce has roughly half the sodium of regular soy sauce. Bragg Liquid Aminos is made from unfermented soybeans and contains essential and nonessential amino acids. It has slightly less sodium than regular soy sauce, and may be used as a substitute.

Nuts and Seeds

Good news for nut lovers: Nuts do more than add texture and hearty flavor to meatless meals like salads, veggie burgers, and pilafs—they also add nutrients. An amino acid in nuts, arginine, helps keep arteries clear. Calcium, folate, magnesium, potassium and vitamin E, all found in nuts, have heart-protective qualities. Even the fat (mostly monounsaturated) in nuts is good for your heart and contains a phytosterol that has anticancer properties.

Some nuts of note: Almonds top the list for calcium, fiber and vitamin E content. Brazil nuts are a rich source of selenium, another anticancer nutrient. Cashews are relatively low in fat and high in iron. Hazelnuts stand out for their level of monounsaturated fat and folate. Peanuts (technically legumes) are protein powerhouses. Walnuts are a good source of cancer-fighting ellagic acid and contain beneficial omega-3 fatty acids.

And when considering the crunch factor, don't forget about seeds, like pumpkin seeds, or pepitas, which are a good source of zinc; sesame seeds, which are high in calcium; and sunflower seeds, which offer iron and protein.

Nuts and seeds do contain some calories, so eat them in moderation. When shopping, buy whole nuts and chop them yourself; small chopped pieces are more vulnerable to oxidation (exposure to air, which can make them stale). Store nuts and seeds in a cool place to help keep them fresh.

WHOLE GRAINS AND GRAIN PRODUCTS

Rice and Other Grains

There's no denying the nutritional benefit—or the satisfying taste—of whole grains. Rice, for example, is a good source of iron, protein and B vitamins. While white rice is milled and polished to remove its bran and germ, whole-grain rices retain these nutritious components, which gives them twice as much fiber, and a good supply of vitamin E. All the rices listed below are available in whole-grain form. In general, whole-grain rices take twice as long to cook as their white counterparts, although quick-cooking brown rice is available.

Arborio is a short-grain rice, native to Italy, that is used for risotto. Because of the composition of its starches, Arborio turns creamy-soft on the outside, while retaining a firm interior.

Basmati is a long-grain rice used in Indian and Middle Eastern cooking. It cooks up fluffy and separate, because it has been aged to decrease its moisture content. Basmati has a delicately nutty, almost popcorn-like aroma and flavor.

Jasmine is a long-grain rice with a lightly perfumed aroma and flavor, produced in Thailand and used in Asian cooking and as a substitute for basmati rice.

Sticky rice is also called glutinous or sweet rice. This short-grain rice is used for sushi and desserts. (It contains no gluten.)

Wild Rice is not actually a rice, but a type of marsh grass. It may be either truly wild or paddy-grown. Wild rice requires a long cooking time, but has a wonderful texture and flavor that are good alone or in combination with other rice or grains.

Other colored rices include Bhutanese Red, Black Japonica, Black Forbidden, Himalayan Red, and Wehani. Each of these is a whole-grain rice, with its own distinct flavor and texture.

Other whole grains provide protein, fiber, B vitamins, and a little vitamin E as well. The bulk aisle is a good place to shop for whole grains, but remember that since they include the oil-rich germ, they can become stale. Shop at a market that has rapid turnover, buy only as much as you can use in a month or two, and store away from heat and light. Listed below are just a few standouts among the many excellent grain choices available.

Amaranth is high in protein and low in fat, and contains calcium, iron, and magnesium. Nutty-tasting amaranth makes good porridge, and the little seeds work well blended with other grains.

Barley is sold as whole grains which have been hulled or pearled. Hulled barley has had only the outer husk removed, leaving the nutritious bran layer intact. Pearl barley has had the bran layer polished off as well, so it's somewhat less nutritious, though also faster-cooking, than hulled barley.

Millet is sold hulled and cooks up fluffy with a mild flavor. Millet is easy to digest and a good source of lecithin.

Quinoa offers excellent nutrition, with a good supply of amino acids. Better yet, it has an appealing nutty taste and a delicately crunchy texture, it cooks quickly, and it works in everything from hot breakfast cereal to pilaf. When picked, quinoa has a protective coating of bitter saponins. Most quinoa sold in this country has been pre-washed to remove this layer, but it's a good idea to rinse quinoa before using it.

Tef is an extremely tiny grain, sold whole with its nutritious bran intact. Tef is high in protein and calcium. Its size makes it suitable as a hot breakfast cereal, and in its native Ethiopia, it is also used to make a bread called injera.

Pasta

With a jar of tomatoes or sauce and a box of pasta in your pantry, you're never more than minutes away from a satisfying meal. Pasta is sold fresh, frozen, or dried; dried pasta is made from a type of wheat flour called durum semolina. If you choose dried pasta made with whole wheat or other grains, you'll get a nutritional boost. Spelt pasta is made from an ancient relative of wheat that's high in protein and easy on the digestive system. Whole-grain spelt pasta has 8 grams of protein and 5 grams of fiber per serving. Other healthy pasta choices are made from brown rice, corn, quinoa, amaranth, or kamut, or a blend of these grains. Be sure not to overcook these pastas; their lower gluten content means they're apt to fall apart unless served al dente (still slightly firm).

In addition to traditional European-style pastas, Asian noodles provide a range of textures and flavors that can dramatically expand your cooking repertoire. Here are a few popular choices:

Bean threads, also known as cellophane noodles, glass noodles, or woon sen, are made from mung bean starch and become translucent when cooked. They are used in soups, salads, and stir-fries and have a somewhat gelatinous texture.

Ramen noodles are thin, curly wheat noodles that are usually fried before being dried.

Rice noodles come in different widths, from rice vermicelli (very thin and thread-like) to wide. Also called rice sticks, ban pho, or sen lek, they're used in Chinese, Vietnamese, Malaysian and Thai cooking. Thinner noodles are used for soups or as spring roll fillings, and thicker ones are used in stir-fries.

Soba, or Japanese buckwheat noodles, have a chewy texture and hearty flavor. Flat like fettuccine, they come in different widths.

Somen noodles are thin Japanese wheat noodles, usually served cold.

Udon noodles are thick Japanese wheat noodles, usually served in soups.

Flour and Sugar

If you like to bake, there are plenty of ways to boost the nutrition of your baked goods, starting with the flour and sugar. Whole-wheat flour is made from the entire kernel of wheat—bran, germ and all. It has more fiber, vitamins and minerals than white flour but also produces coarser, denser baked goods, so you may want to replace just a portion of the all-purpose flour called for with whole-wheat. There are three basic kinds:

Regular whole-wheat flour is milled from hard, or high-protein, wheat and is best suited for yeast breads, where it contributes a hearty texture and robust flavor.

Whole-wheat pastry flour is milled from a soft, or low-protein, variety of wheat that doesn't form much gluten (strong elastic strands of protein) when it's mixed. It's best for cakes, cookies, pies, and quick breads, where lightness and tenderness are more desirable than strength and elasticity.

White whole-wheat flour is milled from a variety of light-colored wheat that gives it a pale color and mild flavor. It has the same protein content as regular whole-wheat flour and is used the same way.

And don't forget **wheat germ**; its nutty flavor and concentrated nutrients make a perfect addition to cookies, cakes and breads, both in the batter and sprinkled on top. Store all whole-wheat flours and germ in a cool, dry place to keep them fresh.

For those with wheat or gluten allergies, or who want to introduce different flavors, textures, and nutrients to their baked goods, you have many non-wheat flours from which to choose. These include barley, oat, rye and spelt flour, which contain gluten or gluten-like substances, and buckwheat, corn, potato and rice flour, which contain no gluten. Low- to no-gluten flours may be blended with all-purpose flour or used by themselves in desserts that don't rely on gluten for structure, such as fruit crisps.

Sweeteners

Most commercial granulated sugar is processed from cane juice using chemicals to bleach it and animal-derived charcoal to remove impurities, which makes it undesirable for people who wish to avoid using animal products. So called natural sugars are minimally less refined and don't use bone char.

Brown sugar is not less refined sugar, but refined sugar with molasses (a byproduct of sugar manufacturing) added back in for flavor and texture. That said, it does contain small amounts of calcium, potassium, phosphorous and iron.

Rapadura and Sucanat are both brand names for evaporated cane juice; sugar that is less refined, leaving more of its natural nutrients intact. These natural sugars are dark beige in color, with a sandy texture and a slight molasses flavor. They can be used cup-for-cup in place of sugar, although they don't dissolve quite as well.

Liquid sweeteners, such as barley malt, brown rice syrup, maple syrup and molasses, are suitable for desserts, although they can't simply be substituted for an equal amount of granulated sugar. Generally, you would use 25 percent less liquid sweetener, and if there is liquid in the recipe, it should also be reduced by 25 percent to compensate for the added moisture provided by the sweetener. Also keep in mind that each liquid sweetener imparts a distinct flavor to baked goods, which is different than the neutral sweetness contributed by sugar.

FRUITS AND VEGETABLES

You've probably heard it many times: Try to eat between five and nine servings of fruits and vegetables every day, and choose them from all the colors of the rainbow. The numbers may sound high but it's really not that hard to achieve. In most cases, a serving is between one-half cup (for berries and chopped fruit and vegetables) and one cup (for raw, leafy greens). As for the rainbow part, shopping for color adds more than just visual appeal to your plate. The same substances that make brightly colored vegetables and fruits so attractive are also responsible for much of their healthfulness. These nutrients are antioxidants; they protect the fruit or vegetable from damage by the sun, and they also protect you from the damaging effects of oxidation.

The fresher the fruit or vegetable, the more of its important nutrients are intact, so shop for local, seasonal produce. (Tropical fruit, while not local for many of us, is a worthwhile exception.) Consider buying organic, at least for heavily sprayed produce such as strawberries and spinach. Look for fruits and vegetables that feel heavy for their size and have taut, shiny skin. Leaves should be brightly colored, not yellowed or washed out. Roots should be firm, not flabby.

Finally, eat a variety of both cooked and raw fruits and vegetables. You'll get a more interesting array of tastes and textures, and better nutrition, too. Some nutrients, like vitamin C, are adversely affected by cooking, while others, like vitamin A and lycopene, are actually absorbed better by the body in their cooked form.

Below is just a sampling of nutritional stars among the huge variety of fruits and vegetables you can choose from, listed with their notable nutrients. The next time you're in the produce aisle, why not pick up a few?

Fruits

Berries Bright, jewel-toned berries are priceless sources of antioxidants. Blueberries, for instance, have the highest antioxidant capacity of any fruit or vegetable. Blackberries offer the antioxidant vitamins C and E and their multiple seeds make them a good source of fiber. Cranberries are perhaps best known for their ability to deter urinary tract infections, but they also contain substances called phenols that help protect your heart. Enjoy berries fresh in the summer, freeze them or buy them frozen for use in desserts or smoothies at other times of year.

Melons Members of the squash family, melons share some of the same health benefits. They're a good source of potassium and vitamin C, and orange-fleshed varieties like cantaloupe and crenshaw have exceptional amounts of beta-carotene, which your body converts to vitamin A. Perhaps the star of the melon family is watermelon; in addition to the above nutrients, it offers iron and a healthy dose of lycopene, a relative of beta carotene that has powerful anticancer properties. A slice of fresh melon is delicious as an appetizer, as part of a fresh fruit salad or as an anytime snack.

Tree Fruits Tree fruits make convenient, portable snacks as well as delicious desserts. Apples are rich in pectin, a type of fiber that may help to reduce cholesterol and maintain steady blood pressure. Eat them unpeeled; their skins contain quercetin, an antioxidant that helps protect your lungs and heart. Apricots, fresh or dried, are high in beta carotene, and provide potassium and fiber. Cherries contain antioxidants that may help to fight inflammation and regulate sleep patterns.

Tropical Fruits   Most tropical fruits are high in potassium and fiber, beta carotene and vitamin C. One large kiwi provides your day's requirement of vitamin C, and a mango gives you a day's worth of beta carotene. Avocados, with their mild flavor and high content of healthy monounsaturated fat, make a great alternative to butter or margarine for spreading on toast. They also contain more folate, vitamin E, potassium and magnesium than other commonly consumed fruits. Pink and red grapefruits contain pectin, a type of soluble fiber that may help lower cholesterol and keep cancer cell growth in check. Half a grapefruit, chilled, forms an ideal part of your breakfast.

Other Fruits   Grapes, especially red and purple ones, contain potent antioxidant pigments called anthocyanins. And all grapes contain catechins, which may help protect the heart, and quercetin. Most of these nutrients are concentrated in the skin and seeds. Children love grapes as a healthy snack which is easy to eat.

Vegetables

Cruciferous Vegetables The large family of cruciferous vegetables includes those that form heads, like broccoli, Brussels sprouts, cabbage and cauliflower, and leafy vegetables like bok choy, chard, kale, collard and mustard greens. All contain sulfur compounds (responsible for a strong smell if overcooked) that have shown anticancer properties in tests. They are also good sources of beta carotene (which your body converts to vitamin A), folate, and potassium. These vegetables are best steamed or chopped into small pieces in a stir-fry or other cooked dish.

Leafy Vegetables   Most lettuces are modest in the nutrition department, although darker-leaved lettuces contain more nutrients than those with pale leaves (notably iceberg). However, many leafy greens used for salad are part of the large family of cruciferous vegetables; as such, they provide a fair amount of nutrients including calcium, folate, beta carotene, and vitamin C. Eating mesclun mix, or spring mix (sold loose or prepackaged) is an easy way to get many of these greens at once; it consists of an assortment of baby cruciferous greens, such as arugula, chard, mizuna, and tatsoi. Leafy vegetables are usually best eaten raw in a salad.

Root Vegetables Root vegetables add heartiness and a satisfying stick-to-the-ribs quality to meals. Beets, carrots and parsnips are rich in anticancer properties and minerals. They can be steamed, baked or roasted. Onions (and their relatives leeks, scallions, and shallots) contain sulfur compounds which may help to keep arteries clear and lower blood pressure. They are usually chopped and included in stir fries and casseroles. Sweet potatoes, baked, mashed or roasted, are a nutritional trade-up from white potatoes.

Squashes Winter squashes, with their orange flesh, are more nutritionally dense than summer squashes and zucchini, supplying beta carotene, iron and riboflavin. Good choices include acorn, buttercup, butternut, delicata, spaghetti, hubbard, kabocha and sugar pumpkin. The common butternut squash is a very good source of dietary fiber. Squash is usually baked but can also be steamed. Most need to be peeled before or after cooking, but the skin of delicata squash is soft enough to eat.

Other Vegetables Mushrooms are more nutritious than you might think. They contain B vitamins, copper, selenium, potassium, and some (like shiitake) are being studied for their anticancer polysaccharides. They are tasty raw in salads, and add a delicious flavor to stews and gravy.

Peppers, especially red and orange, are rich in beta carotene and vitamin C (they have three times the amount, ounce for ounce, of citrus fruit). They can be eaten raw in salads, baked or stir fried.

Tomatoes are a good source of vitamin C. They're also rich in lycopene; cooking makes this cancer-fighting nutrient more absorbable, as does serving the tomatoes with some oil.

HERBS AND SPICES

You can add big flavor to your meals with just a little chopping or a shake of a jar, when you use fresh or dried herbs and spices. Many tender leafy herbs, like basil and parsley, are at their best fresh, while tougher herbs, like rosemary and oregano, hold up better to the drying process. To make fresh herbs last longer, remove the rubber band or twist tie holding them as soon as you get them home, and if you're not planning to use them in a day or two, store fresh herbs upright in a glass of water, like a bunch of flowers. As for dried herbs and spices, remember they have a shelf life too. If a dried herb or spice doesn't smell like itself anymore, it's time to toss it and buy a new jar. If your local food store has a bulk department, check out the bulk herb and spice section. The price is often a small percentage of what you pay for individual jars. Here are just a few of the fresh herbs, spices and spice blends used in the recipes in this book:

Basil is a member of the mint family, frequently employed in Mediterranean and Asian cooking. The more familiar Italian dishes tend to use sweet basil, also known as Genovese basil. Holy basil, a more pungent variety, is used in Asian dishes. If you garden or frequent farmer's markets, you may be familiar with other varieties, such as cinnamon, lemon or opal basil.

Cardamom is a pungent, aromatic spice that belongs to the ginger family. It's used in Scandinavian and Indian cooking for everything from beverages to baked goods to stews. Cardamom may be bought already ground, or in the pod. If buying pods, break them open and crush the small black seeds inside with a mortar and pestle.

Cilantro, also called coriander, or sometimes Chinese parsley, is easy to confuse with flat-leaf parsley. But a sniff or two makes the difference clear. Cilantro's distinctive aroma and flavor is a key element in many Latin American and Asian dishes.

Cinnamon, like cardamom, is equally at home in savory and sweet dishes. The bark of an evergreen tree, cinnamon is sold in sticks or ground. Most of what we buy in the United States is cassia cinnamon, a pungent, reddish brown variety. Ceylon cinnamon is milder and somewhat sweeter. It may be found in Latin American or Indian markets.

Curry pastes are commercially prepared blends that generally contain chiles, garlic, lemongrass, galangal (a peppery spice similar to ginger root) and other spices. They're used to make Thai dishes, and are all fairly spicy although the heat level varies. Common curry pastes include, from milder- to hotter-tasting, Massaman, Panang, Red and Green. Roasted curry paste contains dried chiles, shallots and garlic, as well as other spices, which have been roasted for deeper flavor before grinding.

Curry powder is a commercial blend of spices that usually contains cumin, coriander, chile peppers, fenugreek and turmeric, among other spices. Madras-style curry powder is hotter than standard curry powder. You can customize curry powder by adding your own spices to it, such as ginger or nutmeg.

Garam Masala is an Indian blend of warming spices that generally includes cardamom, cinnamon, black pepper, cloves, cumin and nutmeg. It is often used in lentil dishes, but also goes well with hot breakfast cereals and vegetables such as sweet potatoes.

Garlic helps to promote circulation and may lower cholesterol. A member of the onion family, it contains sulfur compounds, like allicin, that may prevent cancer cell growth. When buying garlic, look for heads with firm, plump cloves and no green shoots. Allicin develops upon exposure to air, when garlic is chopped. To maximize its effect, peel and mince garlic ahead of time and let it sit about 10 minutes before cooking with it. Braise or roast garlic cloves until soft to give dishes a mellow richness rather than a sharp garlic flavor.

Ginger looks like a knobby beige root; generally you can break off a chunk and buy what you need. For convenience, though, you can store ginger in the freezer and grate it while still frozen. A 1-inch piece of fresh ginger will yield about a tablespoon of minced ginger. If you have access to an Asian market, look for young ginger. The skin is translucent instead of papery beige, and the root itself is less fibrous, so it's easier to chop. Unlike mature ginger, young ginger doesn't need to be peeled. Ginger is also sold crystallized, candied (in syrup), and of course, ground.

Paprika is made from a mild, sweet variety of red pepper, which is sun-dried and ground to a powder. There are different varieties of paprika, from sweet to hot (although even hot paprika is not spicy compared to other pepper products). Most recipes call for sweet paprika.

Parsley has a bright fresh flavor that's a necessity in tabbouleh, bouquet garni, and many other European and Mediterranean dishes. Most supermarkets offer both flat-leaf and curly parsley; the former is the stronger-tasting of the two.

Turmeric lends its intense orange color to curry powder, mustard and pickles. It comes from a rhizome related to ginger; when shopping in Asian markets, you may occasionally see turmeric in its root form. Usually, though, it's sold powdered. Turmeric has a bitter flavor and should be used in small amounts.

OILS AND VINEGARS

A drizzle of oil is a nice finishing touch for many dishes, and it's a healthy alternative to butter (or margarine) on vegetables, bread and rice. Ask ten experts, though, which oil is best to use in cooking, and you may get ten different answers. Some believe that the fat composition of an oil is the determining factor in its healthfulness, while others believe that the level of processing, or refining, done to an oil is more significant. In addition, some oils are more suited for some types of cooking than others because of their varying smoke points (the temperature at which an oil begins to smoke and unhealthy compounds are formed.) In general, unrefined oils, those which have not been chemically stripped of color and flavor, have lower smoke points and should not be used in high-heat cooking methods. (For example, the smoke point of unrefined peanut oil is 320 degrees versus 440 degrees for refined peanut oil.) In addition, they have shorter shelf lives and should be protected from heat and light during storage.

Some other general rules of thumb

Oils from nuts and seeds, such as walnut oil or flaxseed oil, are best used for salads or for baking, where they are not exposed to direct high heat.

Sesame oil is sold in light and dark versions; the dark oil is made from roasted sesame seeds and has a stronger flavor and a low smoke point; it is best used as a flavoring in sauces or drizzled over stir-fry ingredients in the last minute of cooking.

Any unrefined oil, including extra-virgin olive oil, is also best used in low- or no-heat dishes. Since unrefined oils tend to be more expensive, it makes sense to use them in ways that allow you to appreciate their flavor. Olive oil not labeled extra-virgin is more refined and better able to withstand higher temperatures.

Among refined oils, those that have been processed to remove their natural flavor, use canola, grapeseed, peanut, safflower, soybean (which is sometimes labeled as vegetable oil), or sunflower oil in higher-heat cooking.

Vinegar is good for more than just salad dressing—it's a low-sodium, low-calorie flavor builder that can enhance a wide range of vegetarian dishes. Add zip to your meals with some of these vinegars:

Balsamic vinegar is made from wine grapes that have been aged in barrels over a period of years. True balsamic vinegar is rich and syrupy—and extremely expensive. Supermarket balsamic-type vinegars may include red wine vinegar and caramel color, but can be tasty. Drizzle *tradizionale* balsamic (the real thing) over strawberries.

Cider vinegar is made from apples, which give it a mild but tangy and fruity flavor. Use in pickles, cole slaw, or stir a spoonful into a glass of seltzer.

Malt vinegar is made from unhopped beer or malted barley. A classic condiment with English "chips" (French fries), it may also be used in potato salad.

Rice vinegar is made from white or brown rice, while rice wine vinegar is made from sake. Both are mild and almost sweet; good for low-fat dressings (because you need less oil to offset their flavor) or for dipping sauces.

Sherry vinegar is made from sherry wine that has been aged in oak barrels. It's less sweet but just as complex as balsamic vinegar. Sherry vinegar makes a splash in soups like black bean, split pea, or gazpacho.

Wine vinegar may be made from table wine or varietals like chardonnay and cabernet. White wine vinegars are milder than reds but both are fairly acidic. Sprinkle on steamed vegetables.

Breakfast
and Beverages

Granola

Chef Dawn Hainey

Editor, Culinary Instructor, Arlington, WA
Recipe from *Taste and See,* published by Cooks by Morris Press

Although this recipe calls for six-grain cereal, you can use any multigrain hot cereal mix; choose your favorite. This granola stores well in an airtight container.

Makes 17 cups

6 cups old-fashioned (regular rolled) oats	¾ cup oil
3 cups six-grain cereal	¾ teaspoon salt
3 cups quick oats	½ cup pure maple syrup or ½ cup brown sugar
¾ cup sliced almonds	
2 cups coconut	2 tablespoons maple flavoring or vanilla
1¼ cups water	2 cups raisins

Preheat the oven to 225°F. Place the old-fashioned oats and six-grain cereal in a food processor and process to a flour; place in a large bowl. Add the quick oats, the sliced almonds and coconut and stir to blend. In a separate bowl or large liquid measuring cup, whisk together the water, oil and salt, then add the maple syrup and maple flavoring and whisk thoroughly. Pour the liquid ingredients over the dry ingredients and stir well, until the mixture is equally moistened. Bake, stirring once or twice, until completely dry and golden brown, 45 to 60 minutes. Remove from the oven and add the raisins. Cool completely before storing.

Reprinted with permission

Vegan Pumpkin Bread

Chef John Koch

Cooks Kitchen Organic Foods
PO Box 1222, Ashland, OR (541) 535-3663
www.cookskitchen.net

The combination of whole-wheat pastry flour and regular whole-wheat flour gives this moist bread a hearty but not too dense texture.

Makes 1 standard loaf

1¾ cups whole-wheat pastry flour	1 (15-ounce) can pureed pumpkin
½ cup whole-wheat flour	¾ cup brown rice syrup
2½ teaspoons baking powder	2½ tablespoons macadamia nut oil or vegetable oil
½ teaspoon baking soda	1 tablespoon lemon juice
½ teaspoon ground allspice	1 tablespoon apple juice
¼ teaspoon ground cinnamon	1 teaspoon vanilla
¼ teaspoon salt	

Preheat the oven to 350°F. Lightly oil a 9 by 5-inch loaf pan. In a medium bowl, sift together both flours, the baking powder, baking soda, allspice, cinnamon and salt. In a large bowl, whisk together the pumpkin, rice syrup, oil, apple and lemon juices and vanilla. Add the dry ingredients to the wet ingredients and stir just until incorporated, being careful not to overmix. Pour into the prepared loaf pan and bake until the loaf is golden brown and a toothpick inserted in the center comes out with just a few moist crumbs clinging to it, about 1 hour and 10 minutes. Let cool before slicing.

Fabulous Spelt Muffins

Oceana Natural Foods Cooperative
159 SE 2nd Street, Newport, OR (541) 265-3893
www.oceanafoods.org

We are famous for our fabulously awesome wheat-free vegan spelt muffins. We make two dozen every morning and always sell out! We enjoy creating unusual flavor combinations to keep our customers happy and healthy…Oceana Natural Foods Co-op

Makes 24 standard or 12 giant muffins

3 cups spelt flour	2 large, ripe bananas, cut in chunks
1 cup rolled oats, plus more for sprinkling on muffins	½ cup soy or grain milk
	½ cup safflower oil
1 tablespoon ground cinnamon, nutmeg, or ginger or grated lemon zest	3 tablespoons lemon juice
	1 tablespoon vanilla
2½ teaspoons baking powder	1 tablespoon lecithin granules
½ teaspoon baking soda	1½ cups chopped walnuts, other nuts, or dried fruit, or a combination
½ teaspoon sea salt	

Preheat the oven to 350°F. Grease two standard or one large muffin pan.
In a large bowl, whisk together the spelt flour, oats, cinnamon, baking powder, baking soda and salt. Place the bananas, soymilk, oil, lemon juice, vanilla and lecithin granules in a food processor and process until smooth. Pour the wet ingredients into the dry ingredients and stir until just a few traces of flour remain, then add the fruit or nuts and stir gently just until completely blended.

Fill each muffin cup almost to the top with batter (an ice cream scoop works well for this) and garnish the tops with oats. Bake until a toothpick inserted in one of the muffins comes out with just a few moist crumbs clinging to it, about 20 minutes for standard muffins, a few minutes longer for large ones. Eat warm or at room temperature.

Chef's Tip
You can substitute other fruits for the bananas and other nuts or fruit for the walnuts in this recipe. Try pureed pumpkin with cranberries (fresh or dried) and pecans. Or peaches with almonds. Or grated carrots and apples with raisins. Vary the spices to suit your taste, too.

Bodacious Breakfast Scramble

Holy Cow Café

EMU Building C at the University of Oregon, Eugene, OR (541) 346-2562
www.holycowcafe.com

A hearty stand-in for Southwestern scrambled eggs—without the cholesterol. Serve this delicious scramble with home fries or tuck it into warmed tortillas.

Serves 3 to 4

- 3 tablespoons tamari
- 3 tablespoons tahini
- 3 medium onions, chopped
- 1 tablespoon olive oil
- 3 medium cloves garlic, minced
- 1 small zucchini, diced
- ½ large red or green bell pepper, diced

- ⅔ cup peas, fresh or thawed frozen
- 1 package (14–16 ounces) firm tofu, crumbled
- 1 teaspoon curry powder
- ½ teaspoon ground cumin
- 2 tablespoon chopped fresh cilantro

In a small bowl, whisk together the tamari and tahini and set aside. Heat the olive oil in a large skillet, preferably nonstick, over medium heat. Add the onions and sauté until soft, about 5 minutes. Add the garlic, zucchini, bell pepper and peas and sauté for 5 minutes. Add the tofu, curry powder and cumin and sauté for 5 minutes. Add the tamari-tahini mixture to the vegetables and tofu and heat through. Remove from heat, add the cilantro, briefly stir to blend, and serve.

Tempeh Bacon

Chef Cynthia Lair

Author, Presenter at Vegfest
Nutrition faculty member at Bastyr University
Recipe from *Feeding the Whole Family*, published by Moon Smile Press
www.feedingfamily.com

Simple and tasty, this seasoned tempeh can be used to accompany pancakes or turned into a vegetarian "TLT" sandwich.

Serves 4 to 6

½	teaspoon dried oregano
½	teaspoon dried thyme
½	teaspoon dried basil
¼	cup high-oleic safflower oil, or organic canola oil
1	(8-ounce) package tempeh, cut crosswise into ¼-inch-wide strips
1	tablespoon tamari or shoyu

In a small bowl, thoroughly stir together the oregano, thyme, and basil. Line a dinner plate with a paper towel and set near the stove. Heat a 10-inch skillet over medium-high heat, add 2 tablespoons of the oil, then half of the tempeh strips. Fry the slices briefly, about 30 seconds on each side. Sprinkle half of the herb mixture over the tempeh as it fries. Remove the tempeh slices and place them on the prepared plate. Repeat the process with the remaining oil, tempeh and herbs. When finished, sprinkle the fried tempeh with the tamari and serve.

Reprinted with permission

Soysage

D'Anna's Deli Café

1307 11th Street, Bellingham, WA (360) 752-3390

Freezing tofu makes it spongy, helping it to absorb flavors, and giving it a firmer texture. For an Italian version, replace the sage and coriander with equal amounts of fennel and oregano, and use rosemary instead of mace. The Soysage will keep fresh for 3–4 days. They freeze well too.

Makes 24 pieces

3 packages (14–16 ounces) firm tofu, 2 frozen, 1 not frozen, all squeezed dry	1½ teaspoons dried sage
1 cup whole wheat flour	1½ teaspoons dried thyme,
6 tablespoons olive or canola oil	1½ teaspoons dried savory
½ cup soy sauce	1½ teaspoons ground coriander
1½ teaspoons ground black pepper	¾ teaspoon ground mace

Preheat the oven to 400°F. Oil a large baking sheet and set aside. Break up the tofu into a large bowl and add the flour, oil, soy sauce, pepper, sage, thyme, savory, coriander and mace. Using your hands, mix and knead the mixture to make it stick together. Spread in a half sheet pan, 9 by 13-inches. Bake for 30 to 45 minutes. Slice into 24 pieces.

Cashew French Toast

Chef Dawn Hainey

Editor, Culinary instructor, Arlington, WA
Recipe from *Taste and See,* published by Cooks by Morris Press

Serve this delicious and unusual French toast with fresh fruit topping, like strawberries or raspberries (lightly crushed and sweetened), or your favorite fruit-sweetened syrup.

Serves 4

- 2   cups water
- 1   cup raw cashews, well rinsed
- ¼   cup pitted dates
- 2   tablespoons frozen orange juice concentrate, thawed
- 1   teaspoon ground coriander
- 1   teaspoon vanilla extract
- 2   tablespoons unsweetened coconut (optional)
- 12 slices whole-wheat bread

Preheat the oven to 400°F. Lightly oil a large, shallow casserole dish or rimmed baking sheet. Place the water, cashews, dates, orange juice concentrate, coriander, vanilla, salt and coconut, if using, in a blender. Blend until creamy (the batter will be thick, somewhat like pancake batter). Pour the mixture into a wide, shallow bowl. Dip the bread slices gently into the cashew cream, being sure both sides of each slice are thinly but thoroughly coated. Use a knife to spread the batter on the bread if that makes it easier.

Place the coated bread slices in the prepared dish and bake until golden brown on the underside, 8 to 12 minutes. Turn the slices and brown the other side, 5 to 8 minutes. If you like, place the bread slices under the broiler for a few seconds for a golden brown crust. Watch closely to make sure it doesn't get too brown. Serve warm.

Mandarin Pancakes

Debra Wasserman
Author, Co-director of Vegetarian Resource Group
Recipe from *Conveniently Vegan,* published by Vegetarian Resource Group
www.vrg.org

Enjoy these uniquely flavored pancakes simply dusted with a little powdered sugar.

Makes 5 large or 10 small pancakes

- 2 cups unbleached white flour
- 1 tablespoon egg replacer *(see below)*
- 2 teaspoons baking powder
- 1 (10½-ounce) can mandarin oranges, including juice
- 1 cup water
  Canola oil

In a medium bowl, whisk together the flour, egg replacer and baking powder. Add the orange sections and their juice and the water, and stir just until blended. Heat a large nonstick skillet or griddle over medium heat and oil it lightly. Ladle the batter onto the skillet and cook until done, about 5 minutes for the first side, a little less time for the second side. Serve warm.

Egg Replacer
One of the healthiest ways to replace eggs in traditional recipes is made from a tablespoon of ground flaxseed added to 3 tablespoons boiling water. Let the mixture sit for 15 minutes then whisk with a fork. This will replace one egg in any recipe where the egg is used as a binder. When a raising agent is needed, 1 teaspoon baking soda and 1 teaspoon baking powder can be added. Ener-G Egg Replacer is a commercial product based on potato starch, tapioca flour and leavening agents, which is also effective. ¼ cup of silken tofu can also be used as a good egg substitute. Be willing to experiment with these options to find the choice which works best for you.

Kasha Varnishkes

Patty Pan Grill

5402 20th Avenue NW, Seattle, WA, (206) 782-1558
Vegfest Chef Devra Gartenstein
Recipe from *The Accidental Vegan,* published by The Crossing Press

This was one of my favorite foods when I was a child….Devra Gartenstein

Serves 4

1	tablespoon olive oil
½	onion, chopped
6–8	mushrooms, sliced
1	cup buckwheat groats *(roasted or unroasted—see below)*
2	cups vegetable broth or water
½	cup bow tie pasta (farfalle)
1	teaspoon sea salt
1	teaspoon chopped fresh parsley

Heat the oil in medium saucepan, over medium heat, add the onion and mushrooms, and sauté until the vegetables are softened, about 5 minutes. Add the buckwheat groats, stir, and cook another 2 minutes. Add the broth, bring it to a boil, then add the pasta and salt and cook until the liquid is absorbed, about 20 minutes. Stir in the parsley and serve.

———

Kasha

Kasha is the name for roasted kernels (or groats) of buckwheat. Buckwheat, actually not a grain but a distant relative of rhubarb, has a distinctive, hearty taste (familiar to many in the form of buckwheat pancakes). When roasted, buckwheat takes on a deeper, almost nutty flavor. Both kasha and unroasted groats may be sold whole or cracked, and buckwheat is also sold as flour. Whichever form you buy, purchase buckwheat from a store that has a high turnover, to ensure freshness.

Fruit Smoothie

Marilyn Joyce, RD, PhD

Presenter at Vegfest, International Speaker, Author, Consultant
Recipe from *I Can't Believe it's Tofu!*, published by Marilyn Joyce
www.marilynjoyce.com

You can use other fresh fruits in season, such as peaches, pineapple, nectarines, mango, papaya, kiwi, pears, cantaloupe, etc. Be adventurous!

Serves 1

4   ounces (½ cup) silken tofu
½   cup vanilla soymilk
½   cup frozen strawberries
1   large banana

Place all the ingredients in a blender and puree until smooth and creamy. Serve.

Reprinted with permission

Mango Lassi *Indian*

Pabla Indian Cuisine

364 Renton Center Way SW, Renton, WA (425) 228-4625
www.pablacuisine.com

Very fresh and cooling! In addition to mango, you can use any fruit, such as banana, strawberry, etc.

Serves 2

- 2 cups ice cubes
- 1 cup mango pulp
- ¾ cup plain soy yogurt
- 4 teaspoons sugar

Combine all the ingredients in a blender, and blend until frothy, about 1 minute. Serve.

Masala Chai Tea *Indian*

Pabla Indian Cuisine
364 Renton Center Way SW, Renton, WA (425) 228-4625
www.pablacuisine.com

This exotic blend of tea may be served at breakfast, after dinner, and on special occasions. It is especially comforting on cold winter days! Chai masala is a blend of spices sold at Indian markets; it usually contains cardamom, cinnamon, cloves, ginger, nutmeg and pepper.

Serves 4

  4 cups water
¾–1 teaspoon chai masala
  3 bags black tea, any variety
1½ cups soymilk
  1 tablespoon sugar, or to taste

Place the water, chai masala, and tea bags in a medium saucepan, bring to a boil over medium heat and simmer for 5 minutes. Add the soymilk and sugar, and simmer for another 3 to 5 minutes. Strain and serve hot.

Appetizers

Bruschetta *Italian*

The Sixth Street Bistro & Loft

509 Cascade Avenue, Hood River, OR (541) 386-5737

This bruschetta topping can be served in the traditional way on toast, as it is here, or it can accompany a salad or substitute for mild salsa. The topping can be prepared a day in advance and stored airtight in the refrigerator.

Serves 8

    4 Roma tomatoes, diced
    1 green bell pepper, diced
    1 yellow bell pepper, diced
    1 red onion, diced
    1 cup chopped fresh basil
    5 cloves garlic, 3 minced, 2 left whole
    2 tablespoons extra virgin olive oil
    1 tablespoon balsamic vinegar
       Salt and freshly ground black pepper
    1 loaf of country bread, white or whole-grain

Place the tomatoes, peppers, onion, basil and minced garlic in a large bowl, pour the oil and vinegar over them, and gently stir to mix all the ingredients together. Season with salt and pepper to taste. Just before serving, slice the bread, toast the slices until light golden brown and rub them with the whole garlic cloves (the rough surface of the bread will disintegrate the garlic). Spoon some of the bruschetta topping onto the toast slices and serve.

Tuscan Hummus *Italian*

California Pizza Kitchen
401 Northgate Way, Seattle, WA (206) 367-4445

"Yummus" is how counter server Hayle Ohman describes this appetizer to her customers. What makes this version uniquely Italian is its use of white beans instead of the traditional garbanzo beans. For those who might enjoy an extra-zesty flavor, accompany the dip with lemon wedges to squeeze. Vegetables, such as cherry tomatoes, are also good for dipping…California Pizza Kitchen

Makes about 4 cups

8–10 medium cloves garlic
 2 (15-ounce) cans cannellini or
    Great Northern beans, drained
 ½ cup tahini
 6 tablespoons extra-virgin olive oil
 ¼ cup freshly squeezed lemon juice
 1 tablespoon plus ½ teaspoon soy sauce

1½ teaspoons salt
1½ teaspoons ground cumin
 ½ teaspoon cayenne pepper
 ⅛ teaspoon ground coriander
¼–½ cup cold water
 8 loaves pita bread
 2 tablespoons minced fresh parsley

In a food processor, finely mince the garlic cloves, stopping the processor occasionally to scrape down the sides of the bowl. Add the beans and pulse the machine a few times to chop them coarsely. Then, with the machine running, puree them while you slowly pour the sesame paste through the feed tube. Still with the motor running, pour the olive oil, lemon juice, and soy sauce through the feed tube, stopping the processor occasionally to scrape down the sides of the bowl.

Stop the processor, open the lid, and add the salt, cumin, cayenne and coriander. Process until thoroughly blended. If the puree seems too thick for dipping or spreading, slowly add the water as needed. Transfer the puree to a bowl, cover with plastic wrap, and refrigerate to chill well before serving.

Preheat the oven to 250°F. Put the pita breads in the oven and heat until thoroughly warmed, 6 to 8 minutes. Carefully remove and cut into wedges. Place the chilled hummus in a serving plate or bowl, garnish with the chopped parsley and surround with the pita triangles. Serve immediately.

Hummus   *Middle Eastern*

Mezé
935 6th Street South, Kirkland, WA (425) 828-3923

Serve this traditional hummus as a dip with raw vegetables, or stuffed into pita pockets with spicy sprouts.

Makes about 4 cups

  2 (15-ounce) cans garbanzo beans, drained
  2 heaping tablespoons tahini
  6 cloves garlic, chopped
  ½ cup olive oil
  ½ cup lemon juice
      Pinch cayenne pepper
      Salt and ground black pepper
  ¼ cup water

Place the beans, tahini, garlic, olive oil and lemon juice in a food processor and puree until smooth. Add the cayenne pepper, salt and black pepper to taste. If the mixture seems too thick, add the water and puree.

Chef's Tip
Although Hummus is traditionally served as an appetizer, it also makes a terrific light main course for four people. Top it with corn kernels, black beans, shredded carrots, sun-dried tomatoes, chopped baby spinach, shredded jicama, and chopped red onion, and use pita wedges to scoop up the mixture.

Mushroom Paté *Syrian*

Pilaf Restaurant

18 Calle Guanajuato, Ashland, OR, (541) 488-7898
www.pilafrestaurant.com

Use as a filling in moussaka, cannelloni, or stuffed vegetables, as a sausage-like topping for pizza, or simply as a spread for sandwiches, crackers, or crostini.

Makes 2 cups

4 tablespoons extra virgin olive oil	2 tablespoons tomato paste
½ medium onion, diced, then minced in a food processor	1 tablespoon oregano
1 tablespoon fennel seeds	2 teaspoons smoked paprika (pimenton)
1 teaspoon Aleppo pepper *(see below)*	Salt and ground black pepper
1 pound button mushrooms, minced in a food processor, half at a time	1 cup fresh bread crumbs (about 2 slices bread)

Heat a large cast iron skillet or other heavy-bottomed sauté pan over medium heat, add 3 tablespoons of the olive oil and heat until it shimmers. Add the onion, fennel seeds, and pepper and sauté until the seeds are toasty and the onion is brown. Add the mushrooms and continue to cook over moderately high heat, stirring frequently. Cook until all moisture is removed from the mushrooms and they are an even brown in color.

Push them to the side of the pan, add the remaining tablespoon of olive oil to the center of the pan and sizzle the tomato paste in the olive oil for a few seconds, then add the oregano and paprika. Incorporate into the mushrooms. Add salt and pepper to taste and the bread crumbs. Stir well, lower the heat, and cook briefly to meld the crumbs into the mushrooms. Press into a small bowl, cover, and refrigerate.

Aleppo Pepper

The city of Aleppo, located in northern Syria, is considered by many as the Mecca of Middle Eastern cooking. The ground red pepper from Aleppo is coarse, dark red, earthy and robust with a mild, rich heat. This pepper is used in most Syrian dishes, especially soups and salads. It is available in Middle Eastern markets. Use cayenne sparingly as a substitute.

Walnut and Pomegranate Spread *Muhamarra, Syrian*

Pilaf Restaurant

18 Calle Guanajuato, Ashland, OR, (541) 488-7898
www.pilafrestaurant.com

This beautiful brick-colored spread from Syria is rich in vitamin C from the peppers, omega-3s and protein from the walnuts, and antioxidants from the pomegranate. It's a gorgeous appetizer garnished with kalamata olives and parsley or as a topping for crostini. Or try it with potatoes or pasta.

Makes 2 cups

1	cup walnuts, lightly toasted
1	cup dry bread crumbs
1	teaspoon smoked paprika
1	teaspoon Aleppo pepper
½	teaspoon salt
3	red bell peppers, roasted and peeled, or 2 cups jarred roasted peppers
¼–½	cup extra virgin olive oil
1	tablespoon pomegranate molasses, or more to taste *(see below)*

Put the walnuts, bread crumbs, paprika, Aleppo pepper and salt in a food processor and blend until a smooth paste forms. Add the peppers and continue processing until smooth, then drizzle in the oil and pomegranate. Stop and scrape the sides of the bowl and adjust the seasonings to taste.

Pomegranate Molasses

Pomegranate molasses is a tart, thick concentrate of pomegranate juice. It has a wonderful flavor and its thickness and dark color make food look very appealing. It blends well with walnuts, adds a tart, pungent flavor to beans and gives a sharp edge to salads and vegetables. It can also be diluted and used for sharp drinks and tart sorbets. It is available in Middle Eastern markets.

Tofu and Jicama Summer Rolls with Sweet and Sour Garlic Sauce *Por Pia Sod, Thailand*

Chef Pranee Halvorsen

Presenter at Vegfest and Monthly Dining Event chef
PCC Cooks Culinary Instructor
www.Ilovethaicooking.com

Summer rolls are a Southeast Asian favorite because they're so refreshing and versatile. Throughout Southeast Asia, from China, Vietnam, Thailand to Malaysia, fresh noodle rolls are different in each country. My version uses jicama and fried garlic for maximum impact in both texture and flavor, and I pair the rolls with a seductively spicy dipping sauce. My summer rolls reflect the influence of my hometown in Thailand, and are prepared without the cooked rice vermicelli found in other versions; however, feel free to add them if you like. Sweet chili sauce is sold at natural food stores and Asian markets…Pranee Halvorsen

Serves 10

Sauce
- 4   tablespoons canola or peanut oil
- ½   cup chopped garlic (about 2 heads)
- 1   cup sweet chili sauce
- ⅓   cup vinegar
- 1   tablespoon water
- ¼   cup ground peanuts
- 1   cup fresh cilantro leaves plus
  ¼ cup chopped fresh cilantro
  Salt and pepper

Filling
- 1   cup jicama, shredded
- 1   large red or yellow bell pepper, julienned (sliced very thin)
- 2   medium carrots, shredded
- 8   ounces extra-firm tofu, shredded
- 20   (6-inch diameter) rice paper spring roll wrappers

To make the sauce, heat the oil in a medium skillet over medium heat, add the garlic, and fry until light golden brown. Whisk the chili sauce, vinegar, water, peanuts and ¼ cup chopped cilantro in a small bowl to blend. Add 3 tablespoons of the garlic along with some of the cooking oil, then add salt and pepper to taste. Set aside.

To make the rolls, place the remaining garlic and oil in a small bowl. Have the jicama, bell pepper, carrot, tofu and 1 cup cilantro leaves ready in separate bowls. Select a saucepan with a diameter slightly larger than the spring roll wrappers, add water to a depth of 1 inch, bring it to a boil, and then keep it simmering over medium-low heat. One at a time, place each spring roll wrapper in the water for 5 seconds then remove and set it on a plate.

Place some of the jicama, bell pepper, carrot, tofu and cilantro on the lower third of the spring roll, leaving a 1-inch border. Sprinkle a little of the garlic over the vegetables. Bring the bottom edge of the spring roll up and over the filling, then tuck in the sides and continue rolling until completely wrapped.

Repeat with the remaining rolls. Cut the rolls in half and serve with the sauce.

Spring Rolls Chinese

Food Co-op Kitchen & Juice Bar

414 Kearney, Port Townsend, WA (360) 385-2883
www.foodcoop.coop

These tasty rolls feature a colorful and unusual filling. The next time you make baked sweet potatoes, throw in an extra one and you'll have a headstart on this recipe.

Makes 10

1 sweet potato	½ medium red bell pepper, cut into long thin strips
¼ cup lemon juice	¼ cup chopped fresh cilantro
¼ cup Bragg liquid aminos	10 rice paper shells
2½ tablespoons sunflower oil	
2 medium cloves garlic, minced	
½ medium head red cabbage, sliced very thin	

Heat the oven to 375°F. Prick the sweet potato with a fork, and bake until tender, about 45 minutes. Cool enough to handle, then peel and mash. Meanwhile place the lemon juice, liquid aminos, oil and garlic in a large bowl and whisk to blend. Add the cabbage, peppers and cilantro and marinate for at least 30 minutes. Drain the vegetables. One at a time, soften the rice paper shells in a bowl of hot tap water. Spread ⅓ cup of the vegetable mixture onto each piece of softened rice paper. Pipe or spoon a tablespoon of mashed sweet potato onto the vegetable mixture. Fold the bottom edge of the rice paper up over the filling, tuck in the edges and roll the rice paper to form a roll. Serve with the Secret Dipping Sauce *(below)*.

Secret Dipping Sauce
½ cup tamari
¼ cup lemon juice
¼ cup toasted sesame oil

Combine the ingredients in a small bowl and whisk to blend.

Mochi Wraps *Japanese*

Chef Kati Peters
Presenter at Vegfest
Seattle, WA
www.chefkati.com

This is a simple, nutritious snack, using mochi, a sweet, short-grained, very glutinous rice which is used to make rice cakes. Mochi can be found in Japanese markets, preformed into balls or squares. Quantities are not specified in this recipe—just prepare as much as you like.

Plain brown rice mochi
Shoyu (Japanese soy sauce)
Sheets of sushi nori, toasted *(see below)*

Place small rectangles of mochi in a toaster oven and bake on high until the mochi puffs up, about 4 minutes. Remove them from the toaster oven and place them on a dish. Dip each piece into a small dish of shoyu and wrap with nori. YUMMY!

Nori
Nori is paper-thin sheets of dried seaweed, ranging in color from dark green to dark purple to black. It has a sweet salty taste and it is generally used for wrapping sushi and rice balls. It is very rich in protein, vitamins, calcium, iron and other minerals. It can be bought plain or toasted (yakinori) in Japanese markets and health food stores.

Grilled Rice Balls *Yaki Onigiri, Japanese*

Chef Kati Peters
Presenter at Vegfest
Seattle, WA
www.chefkati.com

What makes these so delicious, is that the outside is crispy and the inside is steamy soft. Quantities are not specified for this recipe—make as much as you need.

White sticky rice, cooked
Salt
Shoyu (Japanese soy sauce)
Rice syrup

Take the cooked rice and add a small amount of salt. Make triangular "balls." Place on a grill if available, or a dry nonstick frying pan will do. Mix the shoyu and some rice syrup and brush on the outside of the rice balls and grill until crispy.

Spicy Nacho "Cheese" Dip *Mexican*

Debra Wasserman

Author, Co-director of Vegetarian Resource Group
Recipe from *Simply Vegan*, published by Vegetarian Resource Group
www.vrg.org

Serve this yummy dip hot or chilled, with crackers, chips or raw vegetables.

Serves 8

1½	cups nutritional yeast
⅔	cup whole wheat pastry or unbleached white flour
2½	cups water
3	tablespoons soy margarine
⅓	cup hot cherry peppers, diced *(see below)*
1	tablespoon mustard
1	teaspoon garlic powder

Whisk the yeast, flour and water together in a medium saucepan. Cook over medium heat, stirring occasionally, until the mixture boils. Add the margarine. Allow to boil for one minute, then remove from heat.

Add the cherry peppers, mustard, and garlic powder. Mix well.

Cherry peppers

Cherry peppers are pod-type peppers which have the shape of a round cherry. They typically measure about 1¾ inches across, and ripen from green to a bright red color. They vary in spiciness from moderately mild to medium hot.

Reprinted with permission

Pineapple Jicama Salsa *Mexican*

Agua Verde Paddle Club
1303 NE Boat Street, Seattle, WA (206) 545-8570
www.aguaverde.com

Jicama, a pleasantly sweet and mild root vegetable, adds a nice crunch to this salsa. This makes a nice side dish with Tacos de Chayote, page 134.

Serves 6 to 8

1	fresh pineapple, peeled, cored and diced fine
1	small jicama, peeled and diced fine
½	red bell pepper, minced
½	green bell pepper, minced
2	scallions, chopped fine
1	cup chopped fresh cilantro
½	cup apple cider vinegar
¼	cup sugar

Combine the pineapple, jicama, red and green bell peppers, scallions and cilantro in a large bowl. Mix the apple cider vinegar with the sugar in a small bowl. Pour the dressing over the vegetables and toss to mix.

Vegan Cilantro Pesto *Mexican*

Columbian Café
1114 Marine Drive, Astoria, OR (503) 325 2233

This is a zippy Latin twist on the classic Italian sauce. Try it on toasted baguette slices, or mix with soy cream cheese for a delicious dip. Fresh cilantro can be sandy; be sure to clean it well before using it.

Makes about 1 cup
  4   cloves garlic, halved
1–2 jalapeños, stemmed, seeded and halved
  2   bunches fresh cilantro, leaves only
  2   tablespoons pine nuts
  ¼   cup extra virgin olive oil

Put the garlic, jalapeños, cilantro and pine nuts in a food processor. Pulse until the ingredients form a paste, scraping down the sides of the workbowl as necessary. Add the oil in a slow drizzle while blending.

Seven-Layer Fiesta Dip *Mexican*

Chef Heather Houck Reseck, RD
Author, Presenter at Vegfest
Recipe from *Fix it Fast*, published by Review & Herald Publishing Association
www.vegetarianadvantage.com

Beware—this dip is habit-forming! It makes a refreshing main dish on a hot summer day. Serve it for a Saturday night social with popcorn and fruit salad. As a main dish, serve it with tossed salad and smoothies.

Makes about 6 cups

1 (16-ounce) can vegetarian refried beans (about 2 cups)	2 scallions, thinly sliced (about ½ cup)
½ cup mild salsa	1 large tomato, chopped fine
1 (12-ounce) carton firm silken tofu, drained (about 1½ cups)	½ cup finely chopped fresh cilantro (about ½ bunch)
4 teaspoons Mexican Seasoning Mix *(see facing page)*	½ cup sliced black olives
	½ cup shredded soy Monterey jack style or soy cheddar-style cheese
2 teaspoons lemon juice	Tortilla chips, pita chips, or
¾ teaspoon salt	fresh vegetables

Stir the refried beans and salsa together in a small bowl. Spread on the bottom of a glass pie plate or shallow baking dish. In a blender or food processor, blend the tofu, Mexican seasoning, lemon juice, and salt until smooth. Spread the tofu mixture over the bean layer. Layer on the scallions, tomato, cilantro, olives and cheese, in the order listed. Serve or refrigerate up to 4 hours. Serve with tortilla chips, pita chips or fresh vegetables.

Chef's Tip
To make a Creamy Tex-Mex Dip, process the tofu, Mexican seasoning, lemon juice and salt in a blender or food processor until smooth. Makes 1½ cups. To make a Fiesta Dip, prepare the Creamy Tex-Mex Dip. Stir in the refried beans, salsa, and ¼ cup chopped fresh cilantro. Garnish with a fresh cilantro sprig. Serve with tortilla chips. Cover and refrigerate up to 5 days. Makes 3½ cups.

Mexican Seasoning Mix

Chef Heather Houck Reseck, RD

Author, Presenter at Vegfest
Recipe from *Fix it Fast*, published by Review & Herald Publishing Association
www.vegetarianadvantgage.com

Delightfully seasons Vegetarian Chili, Vegetarian Tacos, Sloppy Joes, and Seven-Layer Dip. You'll wonder how you ever did without this versatile seasoning mix! This recipe is mild; adjust it to your taste.

Makes ¼ cup

1	tablespoon mild chili powder
1	tablespoon onion powder
2	teaspoons ground cumin
2	teaspoons paprika
1½	teaspoons garlic powder
1½	teaspoons dried oregano leaves
1	teaspoon dried cilantro or parsley flakes
½	teaspoon ground coriander, optional

Combine the ingredients and stir to distribute evenly. Transfer the ingredients to a container; label and date. Store in a cool, dry place. Use within 6 months. Stir contents before each use.

Chef's Tip

Extra-Mild: Omit the chili powder and increase the cumin to 1 tablespoon, increase the paprika to 1 ½ tablespoons, and increase the cilantro to 2 teaspoons. Spicy: Add cayenne or crushed red pepper flakes to taste.

Reprinted with permission

Soups

Potato Corn Chowder American

Patty Pan Grill
5402 20th Avenue NW, Seattle, WA (206) 782-1558
Vegfest Chef Devra Gartenstein
Recipe from *The Accidental Vegan*, published by The Crossing Press

Mashing the potatoes makes this soup creamy, not unlike a traditional chowder.

Serves 6

6 cups vegetable broth or water	1 teaspoon dried marjoram
2 pounds potatoes, chopped, not peeled	1 teaspoon dried thyme
1 onion, chopped	1 teaspoon sea salt
2 cloves garlic, minced	½ teaspoon black pepper
1 tomato, chopped	1 cup frozen corn
1 teaspoon dried basil	

In a medium stockpot, cook the potatoes in the stock or water for 30 to 40 minutes, along with the onion, garlic, tomato, basil, marjoram, thyme, salt and pepper. Take out 2 cups of the cooked potatoes (use tongs or a large slotted spoon), mash them, and then add them back to the stock. Mix well, add the corn, and cook for another 5 to 10 minutes.

Reprinted with permission

Black Bean, Rice & Squash Soup *American*

Chef Barb Bloomfield
Presenter at Vegfest
Recipe from *Soup's On,* published by the Book Publishing Company

The black beans and golden squash provide a nice color contrast in this hearty winter soup. However, other kinds of beans, like kidney or pinto, make interesting variations.

Serves 6

1 tablespoon olive oil	1½ pounds butternut squash, peeled, seeded, and diced
1 head garlic, chopped (3 tablespoons)	1 cup chopped fresh parsley
4 cups water	2 teaspoons fennel seed
¾ cup brown rice	½ teaspoon dried red pepper (optional)
1 bay leaf	3 cups cooked black beans
3½ cups pureed tomatoes, or 1 (28-ounce) can crushed or ground tomatoes	1 teaspoon salt

Heat the oil in a large pot or Dutch oven over medium heat; add the garlic and sauté until soft and brown, about 10 minutes. Add the water, rice and bay leaf to the browned garlic, cover and bring to a boil. Lower the heat to a simmer, and cook for 25 minutes.

Add the tomatoes, squash, parsley and spices to the soup. Return to a low boil, cover and cook for 15 more minutes. Add the beans and salt, and cook gently for 5 more minutes. Turn off the heat and leave covered until ready to serve.

Reprinted with permission

Super Noodle Soup *American*

Veganopolis
412 SW 4th Street, Portland, OR (503) 730-1469

This soup is the vegan version of Chicken Noodle! Homemade vegetarian stock tastes best but canned or boxed broth, or vegetable bouillon cubes will work, too.

Serves 8

- 4 ounces eggless fettucine or linguine noodles
- 2 quarts vegetable broth, homemade or commercially prepared
- 2 tablespoons olive oil
- 1 medium yellow or red onion, cut into ⅛-inch dice
- 2 ribs celery, cleaned and cut into ⅛-inch dice
- 3 carrots, peeled and cut into ⅛-inch dice
- 4 ounces frozen peas
- 1 fresh (preferred) or dry bay leaf
- 4 ounces chicken-style seitan, cut into ¼-inch dice
  Salt and ground white pepper

In a large saucepan, bring 2 quarts of water to a boil, and add salt to taste. Break up the noodles, and cook them in the boiling water for 4 minutes. Drain the noodles, rinse them in cold water until cooled completely, and set aside.

In a large stockpot or Dutch oven, heat the olive oil over medium-high heat and add the onion, celery, carrots, peas and bay leaf. Cook until the onion is translucent, about 7 minutes, stirring frequently.   Add the diced seitan and 1 teaspoon salt, and stir well. Add the vegetable broth and bring to a boil. Lower the heat, add the noodles and salt and pepper to taste. Heat through and serve.

Chickpea Mash Stew American

Chef Dreena Burton

Author, Presenter at Vegfest
Recipe from *The Everyday Vegan*, published by Arsenal Pulp Press
www.everydayvegan.com

You can make this soup, presented at Vegfest, as smooth or chunky as you like, depending on how much you mash or puree it. Serve it with some nice crusty whole-grain bread.

Serves 6 to 8

1½ tablespoons olive oil	2 (14-ounce) cans chickpeas, rinsed and drained (about 3½ cups)
2 medium onions, chopped (about 1½ cups)	1 (28-ounce) can diced tomatoes (do not drain)
2 medium ribs celery, chopped (about 1 cup)	
2 medium carrots, chopped (about 1 cup)	2 cups vegetable broth
3 cloves garlic, chopped	1 cup water
¼ teaspoon sea salt	½ cup sun-dried tomatoes, chopped
Freshly ground black pepper	1 tablespoon tamari
1 medium zucchini, chopped	2 teaspoons molasses
1½ teaspoons dry mustard	1 large bay leaf
¾ teaspoon ground dried sage	1 tablespoon chopped fresh thyme

In a large stockpot or Dutch oven, heat the olive oil over medium heat. Add the onions, celery, carrots, garlic, salt and black pepper to taste. Cover and cook, stirring occasionally, until the vegetables soften, 6 to 8 minutes. Add the zucchini, mustard, and sage, and cook, stirring for a couple of minutes. Add the chickpeas, canned tomatoes and their juice, broth, water, sun-dried tomatoes, tamari, molasses and bay leaf, and bring to a boil. Reduce the heat, cover and simmer 15 to 20 minutes.

Remove but reserve the bay leaf, and mash or lightly puree the soup (keeping it slightly chunky), then stir in fresh thyme. Add the bay leaf back in and simmer for another 3 to 5 minutes. Adjust the seasonings with more salt and pepper to taste, remove the bay leaf and serve.

Cumin Carrot Soup *American*

Nancy Berkoff, RD, EDD, CCE

Contributor to the Vegetarian Journal, published by the Vegetarian Resource Group

This "creamy" soup tastes rich and has a satiny finish.

Serves 5

	Vegetable oil spray
1	medium onion, chopped
1½	pounds carrots, peeled and cut into ½-inch slices
2	teaspoons ground cumin
½	teaspoon white pepper
2	cups vegetable broth
1	tablespoon chopped fresh parsley
	Shredded carrots (optional)

Spray a medium saucepan with vegetable oil and heat over medium heat. Add the onions and cook until translucent and shiny, about 3 minutes. Add the carrots, cumin, and white pepper, and stir to combine. Add the broth, bring to a rolling boil, reduce heat, and simmer until the carrots are very tender, about 15 minutes. Put the soup in a blender or food processor and purée until smooth. Pour the soup back into the saucepan and cook over low heat until heated through.

Garnish with chopped parsley and a sprinkle of fresh, uncooked shredded carrots, if desired, and serve.

Reprinted with permission

Cream of Vegetable Soup American

Marilyn Joyce, RD, PhD

Presenter at Vegfest, International Speaker, Author, Consultant
Recipe from *I Can't Believe it's Tofu!* by Marilyn Joyce
www.marilynjoyce.com

This recipe is very versatile. If you like, substitute other vegetables, such as spinach or tomatoes, for the broccoli and cauliflower. A coffee grinder works well for grinding the oatmeal. Serve this soup with sprouted bread or nonfat, whole grain crackers and a colorful salad.

Serves 2

12 ounces silken tofu	1 tablespoon low-sodium soy sauce
½ cup broccoli florets	4 ounces nonfat cheddar- or
½ cup cauliflower florets	Swiss-style nondairy cheese
½ medium onion, chopped	Plain soymilk, as needed
2 medium cloves garlic	Cayenne pepper
2 tablespoons oatmeal, ground fine	Chopped fresh parsley

Place the tofu, broccoli, cauliflower, onion, garlic, oatmeal, soy sauce and nondairy cheese in a blender, puree until smooth, then blend until creamy. Pour the mixture into a medium saucepan and heat over medium heat just until hot, to preserve the nutrients. If the soup mixture is too thick, add soymilk as required. Garnish with cayenne pepper and parsley and serve.

Chef's Tip

For a dairy-free version of your favorite cream soup, use nut "cream" instead. Cashews work particularly well because of their mild flavor and relatively soft texture, but almonds are very good too. Place about a cup of nuts in a blender with enough water to cover them (or if you're making tomato soup, try tomato juice), and puree until the mixture becomes a smooth paste. Then add more liquid to achieve a creamy consistency. You can start with store-bought nut butters, but be careful of salted ones; too much salt could spoil the soup.
–Heather Burmeister, Cup and Saucer Café, Portland, Oregon

Classic Gazpacho Spanish

The LocoMotive
291 E 5th Street, Eugene, OR (541) 465-4754
www.thelocomotive.com

This chilled tomato soup is a great seasonal recipe. It came from a good cook in Grenada, Spain—it's the real thing! Place the garnish ingredients in small bowls with spoons and serve them next to the soup, so your guests can add what they like.

Serves 4 to 5

Soup
- 6 ounces crustless stale French bread
- 1½ pounds ripe tomatoes (preferably Roma), cored and quartered
- 8 ounces cucumbers, peeled and chopped
- 8 ounces green bell peppers, stemmed, seeded, cut in large chunks
- 8 ounces yellow onions, chopped
- 4–5 large cloves garlic, halved
- 2½ tablespoons red wine vinegar
- 1 tablespoon extra virgin olive oil
- 2¼ teaspoons salt, or to taste

Garnishes
- 1 medium tomato, cut into ¼-inch dice
- 1 small cucumber, peeled and cut in ¼-inch dice
- ½ green bell pepper, cut into ¼-inch dice
- 4 scallions, chopped fine

Preheat the oven to 250°F. Cut half the bread into ¼-inch dice and bake until crunchy but not brown, turning for even baking, 10 to 15 minutes. Soak the other half of the bread in water until mushy.

Squeeze out the soaked bread and place it in a food processor or blender, in batches if the capacity is small, with the tomatoes, cucumbers, peppers, onions, garlic, vinegar, oil and salt. Process to a smooth puree. Empty the batches into a large bowl if doing more than one, and mix well. Taste and add salt or vinegar, if necessary. Chill the soup thoroughly before serving. Chill the serving bowls. Place the diced, toasted bread, diced tomato, cucumber, green pepper and scallions in individual bowls to serve as garnishes with the soup.

Soup à la Tomate *French*

Berry Fields Café
201 S Pearl Street, Centralia, WA (360) 736-1183

This is a soup to make in late summer, when local tomatoes (from a farmers' market or your own garden) are at their ripest and most flavorful.

Serves 4

   1   tablespoon olive oil
   1   small onion, diced
   1   pound fresh tomatoes, diced
   2   tablespoons flour
   4   cups water
   8   fresh basil leaves
   1   tablespoon dried thyme
   1   tablespoon brown sugar
       Salt and freshly ground black pepper

Heat the oil in a large saucepan over medium heat, add the onion and sauté until soft and translucent, about 10 minutes. Add the tomatoes and sauté for 30 seconds. Add the flour and sauté, stirring, for another 30 seconds. Add the water slowly, and stir. Add the basil, thyme, brown sugar, salt and pepper to taste. Bring to a boil, then reduce the heat to low and simmer for about 50 minutes, stirring often. Pour into a blender and puree until smooth. Reheat briefly, if necessary, and serve.

Russian Beet Soup *Borscht*

Chef Julia Terry
Author of *Conscious Vegetarian*, published by Julia Terry

This vibrantly colored soup is full of flavor and nutrients.

Serves 10

2 tablespoons olive oil
2 medium carrots, shredded
1 onion, diced
1 red bell pepper, diced
1 medium head green or red cabbage, shredded
3 medium potatoes, diced
4–6 cups water

1 (28-ounce) can stewed tomatoes
2 medium beets, peeled and shredded
1 (14½-ounce) can lima beans
2 cloves garlic, mashed
3 tablespoons salsa
8 ounces pureed silken tofu or vegan sour cream
1 bunch fresh dill, minced

Heat the olive oil in a large stockpot or Dutch oven over medium-low heat. Add the carrots and onion and sauté for 5 minutes. Add the red pepper and sauté 3 more minutes. Add the cabbage and potatoes. Sauté over medium heat until the cabbage is translucent, about 8 minutes, stirring frequently. Add the water; use 4 cups for a thicker soup and 6 cups for a thinner soup. Bring to a boil and cook until the potatoes are tender.

Add the tomatoes, beets, beans, and salsa. Bring the soup back to a boil, boil for 1 minute, remove from the heat, and stir in the mashed garlic. Let the borscht develop its flavor for at least one hour before serving—it will still be hot enough to serve. Ladle into bowls and top each with a dollop of pureed tofu and a sprinkling of fresh dill.

Tangy Lentil Soup — *Middle Eastern*

Garbonzo's

922 NW 21st Avenue, Portland, OR (503) 227-4196
6341 SW Capitol Highway, Portland, OR (503) 293-7335

This simple, nutritious soup makes a perfect weeknight meal, thanks to quick-cooking lentils.

Serves 8

3	tablespoons olive oil
1	large yellow onion, diced
3	large leaves Swiss chard, stems removed and chopped, leaves coarsely chopped
1	pound brown lentils, rinsed and sorted
1–2	tablespoons sumac *(see below)*
	Salt and pepper

Heat the oil in a medium stockpot or Dutch oven over medium heat. When the oil is hot, add the onion and chard stems and sauté until nicely browned, 10 to 15 minutes. Add the lentils and enough water to cover them by about 1 inch. Bring to a boil, then turn down the heat and let simmer, stirring occasionally, until the lentils are very tender, 30 to 40 minutes. Add the sumac and salt and pepper to taste. Add the chard leaves and cook until they have wilted into the soup, 3 to 4 minutes. Serve.

Sumac
Sumac powder is ground from the berries of a bush which grows wild in Mediterranean areas such as Sicily and southern Italy, and parts of the Middle East, notably Iran. It is a deep red powder, essential in Arabic cooking. It has a pleasantly tart taste, preferred to lemon for its sourness and astringency. It can be found at Middle Eastern markets.

Turkish Lentil Soup

Cyber Dogs
909 Pike Street, Seattle, WA (206) 405-3647
www.cyber-dogs.com

Here is another simple lentil soup. It is brothier than the previous recipe and uses warm spices, such as cinnamon, to add depth of flavor.

Serves 8

2	teaspoons olive oil	2	large bay leaves
1	cup onions, chopped	1½	cups brown lentils
4	large cloves garlic, minced	8	cups water
¾	teaspoon ground cumin	1½	tablespoons balsamic vinegar
½	teaspoon ground cinnamon		Salt and ground black pepper
½	teaspoon ground ginger	2	tablespoons chopped fresh cilantro

Heat the oil in a medium stockpot or Dutch oven over medium heat, add the onions and garlic and sauté until they are translucent, 5 to 10 minutes. Add the cumin, cinnamon, ginger and bay leaves and sauté for a couple of minutes. Add the lentils and water, bring to a boil, and cook until the lentils are soft, about 45 minutes. Season with salt and pepper to taste. Garnish with cilantro and serve.

Red Lentil Soup *Masoor Dal, Indian*

Chef Sid Andersen
Presenter at Vegfest
Masala Maza Foods
www.masalamaza.com

This version of lentil soup, presented at Vegfest, uses red lentils, which cook even more quickly than brown ones and break down almost to a puree when they are fully cooked. The curry powder contributes to the beautiful color and haunting flavor of this easy soup. Serve over basmati rice for a substantial meal.

Serves 4 to 6

2 cups red lentils, rinsed and picked over	3 garlic cloves, minced or pressed through a garlic press
4 cups vegetable broth	1 tablespoon chopped fresh ginger
1 cup water	4 heaping teaspoons curry powder
1 tablespoon expeller pressed canola oil	1 tomato, chopped
1 teaspoon brown mustard seeds	1 teaspoon sea salt
1 teaspoon cumin seeds	¼ cup chopped fresh cilantro
1 red onion, chopped	

Combine the lentils, vegetable broth and water in a medium saucepan. Bring to a boil, lower the heat, cover and simmer for 20 minutes. While the lentils are cooking, heat the oil in a large skillet over medium-high heat. When the oil is hot, add the mustard and cumin seeds (be careful; the mustard seeds should pop). Immediately add the onion and stir for 2 minutes. Turn heat to low and continue to cook until the onion is slightly caramelized (golden in color), about 15 minutes. Increase the heat to medium; add the garlic, ginger, curry powder and tomato and simmer until the juice is cooked off. Add the lentils, salt and fresh cilantro. Let simmer for an additional 5 minutes, and serve.

Persian Barley Bean Soup Ash-e-jo

Chef Omid Roustaei, MA, ABS

Presenter at Vegfest and Monthly Dining Event Chef
Faculty, School of Natural Cookery, Boulder, CO
PCC Cooks Culinary Instructor
www.members.aol.com/wholefoodschef

This filling soup has a wonderful texture, thanks to the variety of grains and legumes it contains, and a fresh taste, thanks to the parsley, cilantro and mint.

Serves 6 to 8

¼ cup olive oil
1 large onion, diced
2 teaspoons salt or more to taste
1 teaspoon ground black pepper
1 teaspoon ground cumin
1 teaspoon ground coriander
½ teaspoon turmeric
½ cup rice
½ cup pearl barley
½ cup brown lentils
5 cups water

1 (14½-ounce) can garbanzo beans
1 cup chopped fresh parsley
1 cup chopped fresh cilantro
1 (10-ounce) package frozen chopped spinach, thawed

Garnish (optional)
3 tablespoons olive oil
4 cloves garlic, chopped
2 tablespoons dried mint
1 teaspoon salt

Heat the oil in a large stockpot or Dutch oven over medium heat, add the onion and sauté for about 5 minutes. Add the salt, pepper, cumin, coriander and turmeric and sauté for an additional minute. Add the rice, barley and lentils and stir to completely coat with the oil and the spices. Add the water, cover, and simmer over medium heat until the grains and lentils are cooked, about 30 minutes.

Add the garbanzo beans, parsley, cilantro and spinach and simmer for an additional 15 minutes. Meanwhile prepare the garnish by heating the oil in a small skillet over medium heat and quickly sautéing the garlic, dried mint and salt for about one minute. Pour the soup into bowls and garnish with the mint/garlic sauce.

Pumpkin Soup with Miso *Gaeng Leang, Thailand*

Chef Pranee Halvorsen
Presenter at Vegfest and Monthly Dining Event Chef
PCC Cooks Culinary Instructor
www.Ilovethaicooking.com

Gaeng Leang is an unknown jewel of Thai soup. This country soup includes fresh seasonal vegetables with herbs and spices, such as shallots, black pepper, Thai chili powder and Thai purple basil. It is enriched with the sweet flavor and smooth texture of kabocha squash. This is ideally served chilled on a hot summer day.

Serves 6 to 8

4 shallots, minced (about ¼ cup)	½ teaspoon ground black pepper
2 tablespoons miso (any type)	½ teaspoon nutmeg
4 cups water	2 dried red chile peppers, ground
1 (14-ounce) can baby corn, halved	into powder or ½ to 1 teaspoon
1 pound kabocha or West Indian	chili flakes
pumpkin or buttercup squash,	1½ tablespoons rice vinegar
peeled and sliced thin	1 teaspoon sugar
10 ounces shiitake mushrooms, stems	2 cups Thai purple basil leaves,
removed, caps sliced thin	washed and torn
1½ teaspoons salt	

In a mortar, pound the shallots together with the miso until it becomes a paste. Put the paste in a large stockpot with the water and bring it to a boil. Stir in the corn, kabocha and mushrooms and boil until the kabocha pumpkin becomes partially translucent, about 5 minutes. Add the salt, pepper, nutmeg, chile peppers, vinegar and sugar, and simmer until the vegetables are tender. Add the basil leaves, simmer for 5 more minutes, and serve.

Kabocha Squash
Kabocha squash or pumpkin is a small, sweet, yellow member of the cucurbit or pumpkin family. In Japan it is known as Kuri Kabocha. It has a nutty flavor and can be found in Asian markets.

Tofu Coconut Soup Tom Kha Tofu, Thailand

Bai Tong
15859 Pacific Highway S, Seatac, WA (206) 431-0893

Even though you don't eat the galangal and kaffir lime leaves in this soup, they infuse it with a spicy, citrusy essence. Both are available at Asian markets, along with straw mushrooms. In a pinch, substitute ginger, a couple strips of lime zest, and small white button mushrooms; although the flavor will not be quite as special, the soup will still be delicious.

Serves 2

2 cups coconut milk	4 ounces straw mushrooms, halved
1 cup vegetable broth	1 tablespoon fresh small green chiles, mashed
10 slices galangal	
3–4 shallots, mashed	3 tablespoons fresh lime or lemon juice
4–5 kaffir lime leaves, torn in half	½ teaspoon salt
8 ounces firm tofu, diced	1 tablespoon chopped fresh cilantro

Place the coconut milk, vegetable stock, galangal, shallots and kaffir lime leaves in a medium saucepan and bring to a boil over medium-high heat; simmer for 5 minutes. Add the tofu and straw mushrooms, bring to a boil again, and season with the chiles, lime juice and salt. Ladle into individual bowls, garnish with the cilantro, and serve.

Galangal
Galangal is a woody root, similar to ginger but stronger, which imparts an aromatic pungent taste to food. It is often used in Thai cooking.

Kaffir Lime Leaves
These leaves add a uniquely refreshing citric, lime-like flavor which is a basis of much Thai cooking. The leaves are too tough to eat (like bay leaves) but are left in cooked food for taste and aroma.

Salads
and Dressings

Mexican Black Bean Salad

Chef Barb Bloomfield
Author, Presenter at Vegfest
Recipe from *More Fabulous Beans,* published by the Book Publishing Company

This salad makes a handy lunch and leftovers are equally delicious the next day. For an especially quick meal, you can use a 15-ounce can of black beans, drained and rinsed. Enjoy the cilantro in this dish or substitute parsley if you prefer.

Serves 6

½	pound potatoes, peeled and diced (about 2 cups)	5	scallions, chopped
2	medium carrots, chopped (about 1 cup)	¾	cup medium-hot salsa
		½	cup chopped fresh cilantro
1	cup frozen corn	½	cup low-sodium tomato juice
1½	cups cooked black beans	2	tablespoons juice from 1 lime
1	red bell pepper, chopped	1	tablespoon olive oil
6	radishes, thinly sliced	1	avocado, chopped into bite-sized pieces

In a medium saucepan, cook the potatoes in boiling water until nearly tender. Add the carrots and cook for 2 to 3 more minutes. Add the corn, stir, then pour the vegetables into a colander. Rinse under cold water to quickly cool the vegetables and stop the cooking process. Drain well.

Combine the black beans, red pepper, radishes and scallions in a medium serving bowl. Add the potatoes, carrots and corn.

Combine the salsa, cilantro, tomato juice, lime juice and olive oil in a medium bowl. Mix well and pour over the vegetables. Toss gently but thoroughly. Before serving, top with the avocado.

Reprinted with permission

Lentil Salad à l'Ancienne *French*

Veganopolis
412 SW 4th Street, Portland, OR (503) 730-1469

A wonderful salad when the weather is cool. The small green French lentils called Le Puy are especially good for salads because they are tender yet firm when cooked.

Serves 4

1¼ cups French green lentils	3½ ounces veggie Canadian bacon, cut into ¼ inch dice
1 small onion, halved	6 tablespoons red wine vinegar
1 small carrot, halved	1 tablespoon Dijon mustard
2 medium shallots, 1 peeled and left whole, the other diced fine	Freshly ground black pepper
2 cloves garlic, peeled	4 tablespoons finely chopped fresh parsley
Salt	
8 tablespoons olive oil	½ cup small croutons *(see Chef's Tip)*

Place the lentils in a medium saucepan, cover them with cold water and bring them to a boil. Skim any scum off the surface and add the onion, carrot, whole shallot, and garlic. Reduce the heat and simmer until almost tender, about 25 minutes. Add salt to taste and cook 5 more minutes. Remove from the heat and set aside.

While the lentils are cooking, heat 2 tablespoons of the olive oil in a medium skillet over medium-high heat and add the veggie bacon. Once the veggie bacon is crisp, remove it from the pan. Return the pan to the heat and add 3 tablespoons of the red wine vinegar, stirring to scrape up any bits of veggie bacon stuck in the pan; remove from the heat and set aside. In a small bowl, combine the remaining 6 tablespoons olive oil and 3 tablespoons red wine vinegar with the Dijon mustard, and salt and freshly ground black pepper to taste, to make a vinaigrette.

Drain the lentils, and remove and discard the vegetables. While the lentils are still warm, season them with the vinaigrette and the reserved vinegar/oil mixture from the sauté pan. Add the veggie bacon pieces and the diced shallot to the lentils and stir well.

Taste for seasoning. The salad should be slightly spicy. Add more black pepper and Dijon mustard to taste. Spoon into a serving bowl or onto individual plates. Top with the parsley and croutons and serve.

Chef's Tip

It's easy to make your own tiny croutons to garnish this salad. Preheat the oven to 350°F. Cut 2 slices of firm-textured bread into ⅛-inch cubes and toss them with a little olive oil and black pepper. Spread them out on a baking sheet and bake them in a 350°F oven until they are crisp and golden brown, about 10 minutes.

Pasta Salad with Asparagus and Tofu *Italian*

Chef Heather Houck Resek, RD
Author, Presenter at Vegfest
Recipe from *Fix it Fast*, published by Review & Herald Publishing Association
www.vegetarianadvantage.com

The tofu resembles feta cheese in this springtime favorite. This dish will accommodate a wide variety of vegetables, like blanched snow peas or broccoli florets, halved cherry tomatoes, sliced bell peppers, zucchini and olives.

Serves 8

½ cup lemon juice
3 tablespoons olive oil
¼ cup grated Parmesan-style nondairy cheese
3 tablespoons minced fresh basil leaves (or 1 tablespoon dried basil)

2 cloves garlic, minced
¾ teaspoon salt
8 ounces firm tofu, drained
6 ounces penne pasta (about 2 cups)
1 pound asparagus, tough ends removed, cut into 1½-inch pieces

Stir the lemon juice, oil, Parmesan-style cheese, basil, garlic and salt together in a large bowl. Crumble the tofu into small pieces with your fingers, add to the dressing and stir to coat. Refrigerate to marinate while assembling the rest of the salad.

Bring 4 quarts of water to a boil in a large pot, add the pasta and salt to taste, and cook until the pasta is tender but firm. Drain and rinse the pasta and set aside. While the pasta is cooking, bring 2 quarts of water to a boil in a medium saucepan, add the asparagus and simmer until crisp-tender, about 3 minutes. Have a bowl of ice water ready; when the asparagus is done, drain it and add it to the ice water to stop the cooking process, then drain again. Add the pasta and asparagus to the tofu and toss to mix. Cover and refrigerate 1 to 2 hours before serving. Refrigerate up to 5 days.

Tofu Salad *American*

PCC Natural Markets
Seven stores in Seattle, Kirkland and Issaquah
www.pccnaturalmarkets.com

Serve this nutritious salad over fresh greens, or use it as a sandwich filling.

Serves 4

Salad
- 1 package (14–16 ounces) firm tofu, crumbled
- ½ cup fresh parsley leaves, chopped
- 2 scallions, chopped
- 1 small carrot, grated
- ¼ red bell pepper, diced
- 2 ribs celery, chopped
- ⅓ cup sunflower seeds, toasted

Dressing
- ½ cup non-egg-based mayonnaise
- 1 cup sweet relish
- 2¼ teaspoons nutritional yeast *(see below)*
- 1½ teaspoons cider vinegar
- 1½ teaspoons white miso
- 1½ teaspoons Dijon mustard
- 1¾ teaspoons dried dill
- 1¼ teaspoons turmeric
- ¾ teaspoon black pepper
- ½ teaspoon salt

Combine the tofu, parsley, scallions, carrot, celery, red pepper and sunflower seeds in a large bowl.

In a small bowl, whisk together the mayonnaise, sweet relish, nutritional yeast, vinegar, miso, mustard, dill, turmeric, pepper and salt to make a dressing. Pour the dressing over the tofu and vegetables and toss gently to combine.

Nutritional Yeast
Nutritional yeast is a dry, granular powder with a cheesy taste, which adds a savory note to sauces, dressings and gravies. It's also tasty sprinkled on popcorn and baked potatoes. Made from the same strain of yeast used for baking, nutritional yeast has no leavening ability because of the way it's processed. It's an excellent source of B vitamins, protein, chromium and selenium. The nutrient levels, notably B_{12}, can vary from brand to brand, so check labels when shopping.

Curried Tempeh Salad

Chef John Koch

Cooks Kitchen Organic Foods
P.O. Box 1222, Ashland, OR (541) 535-3663
www.cookskitchen.net

This protein-packed salad goes equally well on a bed of salad greens or tucked into a pita pocket. It keeps well in the refrigerator.

Serves 8

2   pounds tempeh, cut in small cubes
2   tablespoons vegetable oil
2   cups vegan mayonnaise
4   tablespoons curry powder
1   tablespoon prepared mustard
1   teaspoon vegetarian Worcestershire sauce

¼   teaspoon ground cumin
1   medium red onion, diced small
6   medium ribs celery, chopped
1   cup walnuts, toasted in a dry skillet and chopped
½   cup chopped fresh parsley,

Preheat the oven to 375°F. Toss the tempeh cubes with the oil and spread in a single layer on a large baking sheet. Bake until golden brown, about 15 minutes. Allow to cool. While the tempeh is baking, combine the mayonnaise, curry powder, mustard, Worcestershire sauce and cumin in a large bowl and whisk to blend. Add the onion, celery, walnuts and parsley and stir to combine. Add the cooled tempeh and stir gently until just blended.

Fingerling Potato and Arugula Salad *French*

The LocoMotive

291 E 5th Street, Eugene, OR (541) 465-4754
www.thelocomotive.com

This simple salad makes a light lunch or substantial side dish. Arugula becomes more peppery as it ages; baby arugula is mildly spicy while mature arugula packs a bigger bite.

Serves 4

1½	pounds French fingerling potatoes (or substitute other small, waxy potatoes such as Yukon Gold)
	Salt
4	ounces arugula

Dressing

¼	cup extra virgin olive oil
2½	tablespoons red wine vinegar
1	medium shallot, peeled and quartered
⅓	teaspoon freshly ground black pepper

Place the potatoes in a large saucepan, add enough water to cover by an inch, add salt to taste, and bring to a boil. Cook until fork-tender, about 15 minutes; be careful not to overcook. Drain, chill quickly with ice or cold water and refrigerate until ready to use. The potatoes can be cooked a day ahead.

In a food processor or blender, combine the oil, vinegar, shallot, ¾ teaspoon salt and pepper. If no appliance is available, mince the shallot very fine and whisk the ingredients together, or shake them well in a screw top jar.

Slice the potatoes crosswise ¼ inch thick, leaving on the peel, and place in a large bowl. Add the arugula and most, but not all, of the dressing. Toss the dressing with the potatoes and arugula until they are lightly coated and flavorful, adding the remaining dressing if necessary. Arrange the salad on four salad plates, making sure a few slices of potato show on each plate, and serve.

Salad of Spring Vegetables

Rovers Restaurant

Chef Thierry Rautureau
2808 E Madison Street, Seattle, WA (206) 325-7442
www.rovers-seattle.com

The fresh, bright flavors of spring vegetables are as appealing to the palate as their vivid color is to the eye. Here, they're presented almost like a bouquet of flowers. It's important to use avocados that are ripe but firm: they should "give" just slightly when gently squeezed in your hand. If baby carrots and beets are unavailable, buy the smallest carrots and beets you can find. Cut the carrots in half, then quarter the larger top lengthwise and halve the narrower bottom portion. Halve the beets horizontally, then cut each half into 8 wedges.

Serves 4

Salad

4   ounces baby carrots, trimmed but unpeeled
4   ounces baby beets, trimmed but unpeeled
2   ounces green beans, trimmed
8   ounces fresh peas, shelled (½ cup)
2   ounces snow peas
4   thin spears green asparagus, trimmed
2   large avocados
3   ounces mixed tender greens (such as red oak leaf, green leaf, mizuna, spinach), rinsed and trimmed, large leaves torn in half or quarters
1   plum tomato, peeled, seeded, and cut in thin strips

Garnishes

Red pepper coulis (*see Chef's Tip*)
Yellow pepper coulis (*see Chef's Tip*)
Chervil sprigs
Garlic chive sprigs

Lemon Dressing

2   tablespoons freshly squeezed lemon juice
¼   cup olive oil
Salt and freshly ground white pepper

Bring 2 medium saucepans of generously salted water to a boil. When the water comes to a rolling boil, add the carrots to one pan and the beets to the other; cook until tender, about 7 minutes for the carrots and 20 minutes for the beets. Drain well and set aside to cool.

Refill one pan with salted water and bring to a boil. Fill a large bowl with ice water. When the water comes to a rolling boil, add the green beans and blanch until vivid green and just barely tender, 2 to 3 minutes. Scoop out the beans with a slotted spoon and cool immediately in the ice water. Repeat with the English peas, snow peas and asparagus, cooking each separately until just tender. Lift the cooled vegetables from the ice water and dry thoroughly on paper towels. Cut the snow peas diagonally into thirds. Trim the green beans and asparagus to 2-inch lengths.

For the dressing, combine the lemon juice and olive oil in a small bowl and whisk to blend. Season to taste with salt and pepper, whisking until the salt is dissolved.

Shortly before serving, halve, peel and pit the avocados. Set an avocado half cut-side down on the cutting board and cut lengthwise into 1/8-inch-wide slices, leaving the avocado in place. Use your fingers to gently slide the slices away from one another, forming a long strip of partly overlapping slices, about 12 inches long. Gently draw the 2 ends around to meet and overlap, forming a round "fence" of avocado. Using a thin, wide metal spatula, carefully transfer the avocado "fence" to a salad plate. Repeat with the remaining avocado halves. Drizzle about a teaspoon of lemon vinaigrette over each of the avocado halves.

Combine the snow peas, beans, asparagus and English peas in a medium bowl, drizzle about half the vinaigrette over them, and toss gently. Arrange the mixture in the center of the avocado circle, with some of the vegetables perched up against the edge.

Use your fingers to peel the skin from the carrots and beets. Quarter the carrots and beets, put them together in a bowl, and drizzle with about half of the remaining dressing. Arrange the carrots and beets alongside the green vegetables. Add a small tuft of lettuce to fill out the avocado circle. Scatter the julienned tomato over the salad and add a few sprigs of herbs. Drizzle the remaining dressing on the salad, add dots of red and yellow pepper coulis around the edge of each plate, and serve immediately.

Chef's Tip

Jarred roasted peppers make a quick coulis (thick, pureed sauce); simply drain the peppers, place them in a blender or food processor and puree until smooth, adding salt and pepper to taste. Both red and yellow bell peppers are available roasted and jarred.

Sweet Paprika Potato Salad German

Robert H. Green
Magnolia Vegetarian Cooking Club, Seattle, WA

This salad is equally good served warm or chilled. Make a double batch for your next potluck or picnic.

Serves 4

1½	pounds potatoes, such as Yukon Gold or a similar waxy potato, scrubbed
1	tablespoon extra virgin olive oil
1	large sweet onion, chopped
¼	cup white wine vinegar, or more to taste
1	teaspoon sugar
1	teaspoon sweet paprika
	Kosher salt
1	cup finely chopped fresh Italian parsley

Place the potatoes in a large saucepan, add enough water to cover by an inch, and bring to a boil. Simmer until the potatoes are just barely soft through their centers. Drain. You may peel the potatoes at this point, or leave the skins on if you prefer. Slice the potatoes into thin rounds (about ⅛ inch thick) and place in a salad bowl.

While the potatoes are cooking, heat the oil in a medium skillet over medium-low heat, add the onion and sauté until translucent, about 10 minutes; do not brown. Add the vinegar, sugar, paprika, salt to taste, and parsley. Bring just to a boil. If the dressing mixture seems too thick, add a tablespoon or two of water. Spoon the dressing over the potatoes and stir gently to coat the potatoes evenly with the dressing. Serve warm or cover and refrigerate until chilled.

Marinated Kale *American*

Food Co-op Kitchen & Juice Bar
414 Kearney, Port Townsend, WA (360) 385-2883
www.foodcoop.coop

Lacinato kale, also called dinosaur kale, black kale, or Tuscan kale, is a dramatic-looking vegetable with long, narrow, deeply textured leaves. If you can't find it, you may substitute regular kale.

Serves 4

1   bunch lacinato kale, tough stems removed, leaves chopped
½   small red onion, sliced thick
1   small zucchini, sliced thick
5   cremini mushrooms, sliced thick
1   avocado, peeled, pitted, and cut in small cubes

Dressing
2   tablespoons olive oil
2   tablespoons flaxseed oil
2   tablespoons lemon juice
2   tablespoons shoyu (Japanese soy sauce)

To make the dressing, whisk the olive and flaxseed oils, lemon juice and shoyu in a large bowl. Add the kale, onion, zucchini, mushrooms and avocado, and toss to coat.

Carrots in the Raw *American*

Ashland Food Co-op
237 N 1st Street, Ashland, OR (541) 482-2237
www.ashlandfood.coop

This recipe was developed at the urging of our many raw food customers, but it is equally popular with the omnivore crowd. The ginger gives a bright taste to the fresh, lightly crunchy carrots. As a side dish, it is almost universal in its ability to pair with other foods, from Asian fare to Texas barbecue. Moreover, this is one of those dishes that seem to get better with age. The flavors mesh more sweetly without the salad losing its pleasing texture or vibrant color...Ashland Food Co-op

Serves 6

1¼	pounds carrots, washed, trimmed, and cut into 2-inch lengths
¼	cups seedless raisins
¼	cups raw pumpkin seeds
3	tablespoons extra virgin olive oil
2	tablespoons apple cider vinegar
1½	teaspoons natural sugar (optional)
1½	teaspoons grated fresh ginger
½	teaspoon salt

Cut the carrots on the julienne blade of a food processor or mandoline if you have one. Otherwise, you can use the large holes of a box grater. Place the julienned carrots in a large bowl and add the raisins and pumpkin seeds. Mix the oil, vinegar, sugar (if using), ginger and salt in a small bowl, then pour over the carrot mixture and toss well.

Tomato and Cucumber Salad with Lime-Mint Dressing *Persian*

Chef Omid Roustaei, MA, ABS

Presenter at Vegfest and Monthly Dining Event chef
Faculty, School of Natural Cookery in Boulder, Colorado
PCC Cooks Culinary Instructor
www.members.aol.com/wholefoodschef

Toasted wedges of pita bread make an excellent accompaniment to this salad, which is like tabbouleh without the bulgur.

Serves 6 to 8

¼ cup olive oil
    Juice of 2 limes
1 clove garlic, minced
2 teaspoons salt, or more to taste
½ teaspoon ground black pepper
½ cup chopped fresh mint leaves

¼ cup chopped fresh parsley leaves
4 medium tomatoes, diced
2 cucumbers, peeled and seeded if desired, diced
4–6 scallions, white and light green parts only, chopped

In a large bowl whisk together the olive oil, lime juice, garlic, salt and pepper; add the mint and parsley and stir to combine. Add the tomatoes, cucumbers and scallions to the bowl and toss to coat the vegetables with the dressing. Allow to sit for at least an hour before serving.

Green Papaya Salad _Som Tum, Thailand_

Chef Pranee Halvorsen
Presenter at Vegfest and Monthly Dining Event chef
PCC Cooks Culinary Instructor
www.Ilovethaicooking.com

Som Tum is a country salad from the northeastern part of Thailand. It is served as a side dish with an entrée or by itself as a salad with steamed sticky rice. It is simple and fast to prepare. Thais mix this salad gently with a clay mortar and wooden pestle. Green papayas are sold in Asian markets and many supermarkets. If you can't find one, substitute shredded carrot, cabbage or zucchini.

Serves 4

Dressing
3 cloves garlic
1 Thai chile pepper (optional)
2–3 tablespoons dry roasted peanuts
¼ teaspoon salt
2–3 tablespoons lime juice
1½ tablespoons palm sugar or brown sugar

Salad
2 medium tomatoes, cut into wedges
1 pound green papayas, peeled, seeded and shredded (about 2 cups)
4 ounces green beans, cut in 1-inch lengths

Place the garlic, chile pepper (if using), peanuts and salt in a mortar and crush lightly with a pestle, then add the lime juice and sugar and mix well. If you don't own a mortar and pestle, place the garlic, chile (if using), peanuts and salt in a food processor or mini-chopper and pulse to blend. Add the lime juice and sugar and pulse several more times.

Place the tomatoes, papaya and green beans in a large bowl, pour the dressing over them, and stir, pressing on the vegetables with the spoon to release some of their juices into the dressing.

Quinoa Millet Salad *American*

The Deli Next Door—Skagit Valley Food Co-op
202 South 1st Street, Mount Vernon, WA (360) 336-3886

This is a favorite vegan and gluten-free salad at The Deli Next Door. You can vary the vegetables or add garbanzo beans to make this salad a signature one of your own. Quinoa should be thoroughly rinsed before using.

Serves 6 to 8

5 cups water	⅓ cup sliced black olives
1 cup organic quinoa, rinsed well	1 cup thawed frozen peas
1 cup organic millet, rinsed	
1 cup drained and quartered artichoke hearts	**Dressing**
½ cup julienned carrots	1 clove garlic, chopped
¼ cup diced red onion	⅓ cup lemon juice
¼ bunch chopped fresh parsley	1½ teaspoons salt
½ cup sunflower seeds	1 teaspoon Italian herb blend
	¾ cup light-flavored oil, such as canola

Place 2 medium saucepans on the stove and pour 2½ cups water into each. Bring the water to a boil and add the quinoa to one saucepan and the millet to the other. Cover, reduce the heat, and cook until the grains are soft, about 15 minutes for the quinoa and 20 minutes for the millet. Drain and rinse the grains in cold water. Set them aside to cool.

In a large mixing bowl, combine the cooked and cooled grains with the artichoke hearts, carrots, red onion, parsley, sunflower seeds, black olives and frozen peas.

In a blender, combine the garlic, lemon juice, salt and Italian herb blend. Drizzle the oil into the blended ingredients. Toss the grain and vegetable mixture with the blended dressing and serve.

Chef's Tip
To give this salad an Asian flavor, replace the artichoke hearts with blanched snow peas and the olives with chopped water chestnuts. For the dressing, add 1 tablespoon chopped ginger, change the herbs to an Asian blend, reduce the oil to ½ cup and add ¼ cup toasted sesame oil.

Watermelon, Scallion and Mint Salad American

The Deli Next Door—Skagit Valley Food Co-op
202 South 1st Street, Mount Vernon, WA (360) 336-3886

This refreshing and unusual salad combines sweet and savory flavors. For added pizzazz, substitute champagne vinegar for the white wine vinegar. This salad is best served the same day that it is made.

Serves 6

- 3 pounds watermelon, diced and seeded (6 cups)
- 4 scallions, white and light green parts only, chopped
- 3–4 sprigs of fresh mint, leaves removed and chopped
- 1 small jalapeño pepper, seeded and finely diced (optional)
- 2 tablespoons light vegetable oil
- 1 tablespoon white wine vinegar

Combine the watermelon, scallions, mint and jalapeño (if using) in a mixing bowl. Gently toss the oil and vinegar with the watermelon mixture. Chill and serve.

Lemon Garlic Salad Dressing *American*

Silence Heart Nest
3510 Fremont Place N, Seattle, WA (206) 524-4008

This is a delicious tangy dressing.

Makes about 2 cups

8	ounces firm tofu
6	cloves garlic, chopped
	Juice of 2 lemons
⅓	cup olive oil
1	teaspoon black pepper
½	teaspoon salt
½	cup water

Place the tofu, garlic, lemon juice, oil, pepper, salt and water in a blender and puree until smooth.

Tofu Herb Dressing *American*

Marilyn Joyce, RD PhD
Presenter at Vegfest, International Speaker, Author, Consultant
Recipe from *I Can't Believe it's Tofu!*, published by Marilyn Joyce
www.marilynjoyce.com

Not only does this creamy dressing taste wonderful on salad greens, it perks up steamed vegetables (like broccoli, green beans, and carrots) too.

Makes about 2 cups

12	ounces soft or firm tofu
½	cup organic apple cider
¼	cup white wine vinegar
3	medium cloves garlic, minced
1	teaspoon Dijon mustard
1	teaspoon spicy seasoning salt
½	teaspoon dried basil
½	teaspoon dried oregano
½	teaspoon dried rosemary
2	scallions, finely chopped

Place the tofu in a blender and puree until smooth. Add the cider, vinegar, garlic, mustard, salt, basil, oregano and rosemary, and blend. Pour into a bowl and stir in the chopped scallions. Chill the dressing for about 30 minutes before serving.

Radha Dressing *Indian*

Planet Goloka Organic Grill & Kava Juice Bar
679 Lincoln Street, Eugene, OR (541) 465-4555

Serve this savory dressing over sturdy, spicy greens like mustard and kale. If you can't find asafetida, substitute 1 tablespoon grated white onion.

Makes about 2 cups

1	cup tahini
¼	cup apple cider vinegar
¼	cup lemon juice
2	tablespoons sesame oil
1	tablespoon Bragg Liquid Aminos
2	teaspoons olive oil
⅛	teaspoon asafetida *(see below)*

Place all the ingredients in a blender and puree until creamy and white. Add enough water—up to ¾ cup—to get a pourable dressing.

Asafetida
Asafetida comes from the sap of the roots and stem of a type of giant fennel. It is sold in resinous lumps and as a fine yellow powder. On its own, asafetida has a pungent, sulfurous smell, and an extremely unpleasant flavor, like rotten garlic. However, used in small amounts, it adds an intriguing, onion-like flavor to foods. For obvious reasons, asafetida should be stored well-wrapped, and a little goes a long way. Although the plant is not native to India, asafetida is frequently used in Indian cooking, and can be found at Indian markets.

Garlic Tahini Dressing   Middle Eastern

Olympia Food Co-op
3111 Pacific Ave SE, Olympia, WA (360) 956-3870

When we run out of this dressing, our customers get really mad. Leave out the water and some of the soymilk to make a thicker consistency—use as a dip for raw vegetables or a topping for a baked potato. …Olympia Food Co-op

Makes about 3 cups

>   5   cloves garlic, peeled
>   1   cup toasted tahini *(see below)*
>   ¼   cup lemon juice
>   3   tablespoons tamari
>   1   tablespoon apple cider vinegar
>   Pinch cayenne pepper
>   1   cup plain soymilk
>   ¼   cup water

Place the garlic cloves in food processor or blender and mince. Add the tahini, lemon juice, tamari, vinegar and cayenne. Process to a smooth paste. While the motor is running, slowly add the soymilk and water. Continue processing until smooth and creamy.

Tahini
Tahini is a thick paste made of ground sesame seeds. Toasted tahini is made from roasted and toasted sesame seeds and has a deeper flavor than regular tahini; however, regular tahini can be used for this recipe

Green Garlic Dressing American

Doe Bay Café
Point Lawrence Road, Orcas Island, WA (360) 376-2291
www.doebay.com

This dressing is great for solstice time, or as a good anytime tonic. It's made from the stems and pre-flowering buds of hardneck garlic, called garlic scapes, which are gathered in early summer and sold at farmers' markets. These are delicious! Any leftover garlic scapes can be used in sautés.

Makes about 2½ cups

1	bunch (6 stems) garlic scapes
2	cups olive oil
2	tablespoons shelled flaxseed or hemp seed
1½	tablespoons fresh lemon juice
	Rice syrup (optional)
	Pinch sea salt
½	cup rice vinegar

Cut approximately 4 inches off the bud end of each stem of garlic and chop roughly. (Reserve the lower portion of the stems for another use.) Place the olive oil in a food processor, add the chopped garlic stems, and blend. The greener it gets, the more pronounced the flavor of the garlic. Add the flaxseed, lemon juice, rice syrup to taste (if using), and salt and blend. Slowly pour the rice vinegar into the mixture while blending. It will emulsify and should become frothy, yet thick.

Curry Salad Dressing Asian

Keith Yoshida
Magnolia Vegetarian Cooking Club, Seattle, WA

This is a make-ahead dressing; its flavors meld beautifully when it's allowed to sit a few hours.

Makes about 1 cup

 ⅔ cup peanut oil
 2 tablespoons white vinegar
 2 tablespoons orange juice
 2 tablespoons chutney or Chinese plum sauce
 1 clove garlic, minced
 1 teaspoon curry powder
 ¼ teaspoon liquid pepper sauce or Chinese hot sauce
 ¼ teaspoon salt

Place all the ingredients in a food processor or blender and puree. Chill overnight.

Raspberry Vinaigrette French

Jam on Hawthorne
2239 SE Hawthorne Blvd, Portland, OR (503) 234-4790

Serve this fresh, fruity dressing over salads of baby greens, or cooked grains.

Makes about 2 cups

1	cup fresh raspberries
½	cup chopped fresh basil
½	cup raspberry vinegar
1	large clove garlic, minced
2	tablespoons sugar
1½	cups canola oil
	Salt

Place the raspberries, basil, vinegar, garlic and sugar in a food processor and pulse to combine. With the motor running, slowly add the oil, until the desired thickness is reached. Add salt to taste.

Roasted Garlic Vinaigrette French

Moby Dick Hotel

Sandridge Road, Nahcotta, WA (360) 665-4543
www.mobydickhotel.com

This is a simple and delicious way to add interest to salads. Toss with your favorite greens, cooked vegetables or even cooked, cooled pasta for pasta salad. This keeps well, covered and refrigerated, for a week.

Makes about 1½ cups

- 1   cup olive oil
- 10   cloves garlic
- ⅓   cup red wine vinegar
      Salt and freshly ground black pepper
- 1   tablespoon Spanish sweet paprika (optional)
- 2–4 tablespoons chopped fresh parsley, tarragon or chives (optional)

In a small, heavy saucepan heat the oil and garlic over low heat until the garlic is light brown and soft. Strain the garlic, reserving the oil, and allow both to cool.

Combine the cooled garlic, oil, vinegar and salt and pepper to taste in a blender and run for 15 seconds to puree and emulsify the vinaigrette. If you like, add the paprika or the herbs and puree to incorporate.

Entrées

Barbecued Tempeh

PCC Natural Markets

7 stores in Seattle, Kirkland and Issaquah, WA
www.pccnaturalmarkets.com

This easy recipe makes the perfect weeknight dinner with a baked potato and a salad.

Serves 6

24   ounces soy tempeh, sliced into ½ by 2½-inch strips
1¾   cups barbecue sauce, homemade or commercially prepared
⅔   cup olive oil
1½   green bell peppers, cut into strips
¾   red bell pepper, cut into strips
1   onion, halved and sliced thin

Heat the oven to 350°F. Pour the barbecue sauce into a 9 by 13-inch casserole dish, add the tempeh strips, and toss to coat. Bake for 10 minutes, remove from the oven, stir, and bake until the tempeh is browned and the sauce has thickened, 10 to 12 minutes. Remove the tempeh from the oven and allow it to cool. Meanwhile, heat the olive oil in a large skillet over medium heat, add the peppers and onion, and sauté until softened, about 10 minutes. Add the vegetables to the cooled tempeh, stir to mix, and serve.

Spicy Tofu and Spelt

PCC Natural Markets

7 stores in Seattle, Kirkland and Issaquah, WA
www.pccnaturalmarkets.com

Spelt is an ancient grain (a distant cousin of wheat) that has a robust flavor, is high in protein and easy to digest. Spelt kernels are sometimes called spelt berries and are similar to wheat berries.

Serves 6

⅓   cup tamari
⅓   cup toasted sesame oil
⅓   cup olive oil
2   tablespoons rice wine vinegar
¾   teaspoon cayenne pepper
1   tablespoon grated fresh ginger
3   cloves garlic, minced
24   ounces firm tofu, cut into cubes

1½   cups spelt kernels
¼   purple cabbage (about 4 ounces), shredded
1   red bell pepper, julienned
1   carrot, grated
3   scallions, chopped
2   tablespoons chopped fresh parsley

Heat the oven to 350°F. In a medium bowl, whisk together the tamari, sesame oil, olive oil, rice wine vinegar, cayenne, ginger and garlic to make a sauce. Place the tofu cubes in a 9 by 13-inch casserole dish, pour half the sauce over the tofu, and bake for 20 minutes, then let cool. Meanwhile, bring 4 cups water to a boil in a large saucepan, add the spelt kernels, stir, cover and simmer until tender, about 45 minutes. Drain the kernels, then place them in a large bowl and toss them with the remaining sauce. Add the cooled tofu, then add the cabbage, carrot, pepper, scallions and parsley.

Chef's Tip
You can press tofu to make it firmer and give it a pleasantly chewy texture. Cut a block of tofu in two equally thick slices, put them in large dish, cover them with a piece of plastic wrap, and place a couple of pounds of weight on top (use a cast-iron skillet or a cutting board and place some heavy canned items on it). Let the tofu drain for half an hour while you prepare the rest of your meal.

Southwest Spirals

Ten Mercer
10 Mercer Street, Seattle, WA (206) 691-3723

These pretty rolls are both spicy and fruity. Fresh pineapple tastes best, but you can substitute an 8-ounce can of pineapple chunks, drained, if you prefer. At the restaurant, these rolls are served with a salad of mixed greens drizzled with lemon vinaigrette.

Serves 6 to 8

Salsa

1	orange, preferably organic
1	teaspoon canola oil
1	tablespoon black mustard seeds
4	thick slices fresh pineapple, diced
½	red onion, diced
1	jalapeño pepper, seeded and diced
2	tomatoes, seeded and diced

Spirals

1	jalapeño pepper, seeded and diced fine
3	tomatoes, seeded and diced fine
1	red bell pepper, seeded and diced fine
½	bunch cilantro, chopped
3	scallions, chopped
1	cup vegan cream cheese, softened
¾	cup grated Parmesan-style nondairy cheese
	Salt and ground black pepper
6	(8-inch) chipotle-flavored flour tortillas

To make the salsa, grate the zest from the orange, being careful to avoid the white pith. Peel and section the orange, then cut each section in thirds. In a small skillet, heat the oil and mustard seeds over medium-high heat until the seeds start to pop, 1 to 2 minutes. Add the orange zest and orange sections, then remove the pan from the heat and add the pineapple, onion, jalapeño and tomatoes. Mix well and place in the refrigerator to chill.

To make the spirals, combine the jalapeño, tomatoes, red bell pepper, cilantro and green onions in a steel bowl with the vegan cream cheese and Parmesan-style cheese. Mix well. Add salt and pepper to taste. Place 3 of the tortillas on a work surface and spread a third of the cream cheese mixture on each. Top with the remaining 3 tortillas, press lightly and roll each tortilla "sandwich" up tightly. Wrap in plastic and place in the refrigerator for 30 minutes.

To serve, preheat the oven to 375°F. Lightly grease a baking sheet. Slice the rolls into ¾-inch-wide pieces and place on the sheet. Bake until lightly browned, about 8 minutes. Arrange the spirals on a plate and top with the pineapple salsa.

Spring Pea Garbanzo Pancakes

Café Flora

2901 East Madison, Seattle, WA (206) 325-9100
www.cafeflora.com

These pancakes, presented at Vegfest, make an elegant light lunch, served with Sautéed Vegetable Topping or Roasted Red Pepper Coulis with Gremolata, or both (recipes follow). Chickpea flour is sold in natural food stores and at Indian markets.

Makes about 16 pancakes; serves 4

1 cup frozen peas, thawed, or 1 cup fresh shelled peas	1 cup all-purpose flour
1 shallot, minced	2 teaspoons sugar
3 tablespoons olive oil	2 teaspoons baking powder
2 cups warm water	1 teaspoon baking soda
1 cup chickpea (garbanzo) flour	1 teaspoon sea salt
	Olive oil

Place the peas, shallot, olive oil and water in a blender and puree. Sift the chickpea flour, all-purpose flour, sugar, baking powder, baking soda and sea salt together into a large bowl. Pour the wet mixture into the dry mixture, stirring to remove any lumps.

Heat the oven to 200°F and place a large heatproof platter on the middle rack. Heat a griddle or nonstick frying pan over high heat. Once the pan is hot, lightly coat the pan with olive oil and drop ¼ cup measures onto the pan. Be sure not to crowd the cakes as they will spread some during cooking. Cook until bubbles form, about 3 minutes, then flip them and allow to cook for about 1 more minute; you want both sides of the cakes to be nicely browned. As you cook the pancakes, keep them warm on the plate in the oven, covered with a damp towel so they do not dry out. When all the cakes are done, serve them with your choice of toppings.

Sautéed Vegetable Topping for Pancakes

The fresh flavor of springtime vegetables.

1   tablespoon olive oil
¾   pound asparagus spears, cut diagonally in 1-inch pieces (about 2 cups)
1   yellow bell pepper, seeded and cut into 1-inch pieces
1   cup fresh peas (do not substitute frozen here)
1   cup small cherry tomatoes or 2 medium tomatoes, diced
3   tablespoons white wine or vegetable broth
    Sea salt and ground black pepper

Heat the olive oil in a skillet over medium-high heat. Add the asparagus and bell pepper and sauté for about 2 minutes. Add the peas, tomatoes and wine, cover the pan and cook for 1 more minute. Season with salt and pepper to taste.

Roasted Red Pepper Coulis with Gremolata

Gremolata is a mixture of parsley, garlic and lemon zest. Coulis is a thick puree or sauce.

1   red bell pepper, roasted, peeled and seeded
2   teaspoons balsamic vinegar
1   tablespoon olive oil, plus more if needed
1   tablespoon vegetable broth or water, plus more if needed
2   tablespoons finely chopped Italian parsley
1   clove garlic, minced
½   teaspoon finely minced lemon zest
    Sea salt and ground black pepper

Place the roasted pepper, balsamic vinegar, olive oil and broth in a blender and puree until smooth. Add more oil and broth if necessary to create a pourable mixture. Stir in the parsley, garlic and lemon zest, and salt and pepper to taste.

Warm Endive and Kale Salad with Quinoa Cakes, Beet Caviar and Horseradish Cream Sauce

Café Flora

2901 East Madison, Seattle, WA (206) 325-9100
www.cafeflora.com

The flavors and the presentation of this dramatic dish are sure to impress family and guests alike. It may look complicated, but each component is very easy to put together and much of it can be made ahead of time and stored in the refrigerator until needed. If you like, make the Beet Caviar and Horseradish Cream Sauce and cook the grains and lentils the day before you plan to serve this meal. This recipe was presented at Vegfest.

Serves 4 to 6

Quinoa Cakes
  1   cup quinoa
  ¾   cup millet
  ½   cup black lentils
  4   tablespoons olive oil
  1   shallot, peeled and chopped
  8   ounces cremini mushrooms, chopped fine by hand or in a food processor
  ¼   cup white wine
  1   bunch tarragon, chopped
      Salt and ground black pepper

Place 3 medium saucepans on the stove and pour 3 cups water in each. Bring the water to a boil. Add the quinoa to one saucepan, the millet to the second and the lentils to the third, stirring as you pour. Cover the saucepans, reduce the heat and simmer until tender, about 15 minutes for the quinoa, 25 minutes for the millet, and 20 minutes for the lentils. When each is done, drain and let cool. Heat a skillet on medium high heat, add 2 tablespoons of the oil, then the shallots. Sauté for about 2 minutes, stirring occasionally. Add the mushrooms and sauté for 2 to 3 minutes, stirring occasionally. Add the wine and deglaze the pan by stirring thoroughly to scrape up any browned bits. Allow to cool.

Place the lentils, mushrooms, millet and quinoa in a food processor and pulse just until combined. Turn the mixture into a bowl and stir in the tarragon and salt and pepper to taste. Form into 12 patties. Heat a large skillet over medium heat, add 1 tablespoon of the olive oil and half of the patties, and sauté until brown, about 2 minutes on each side. Repeat with the remaining oil and patties. Quinoa cakes may be kept warm in a 200°F oven, covered, while the warm salad is being prepared.

Beet Caviar

8	ounces red beets, scrubbed		1	small red onion, diced small
3	tablespoons raspberry vinegar		1	tablespoon chopped Italian parsley
1	tablespoon Dijon mustard		1	tablespoon pine nuts, toasted
1	tablespoon ground cumin			

Preheat the oven to 350°F. Place the beets in a small baking dish, add water to cover the bottom of the dish, cover tightly with foil, and bake until just barely tender, 45 minutes to 1 hour. Remove the beets from the oven and increase the heat to 400°F. When the beets are cool enough to handle, peel them, cut them into fine dice and place them in a medium bowl. Add the vinegar, mustard and cumin and toss to combine. Spread the beets on a rimmed baking sheet and bake for 10 to 15 minutes so the flavors can meld. Let cool and combine with the red onion, parsley and pine nuts.

Horseradish Cream Sauce

1 (12-ounce) box firm silken tofu
1 teaspoon sugar
2–3 tablespoon prepared horseradish
2 tablespoon chopped chives

Place all the ingredients in a blender and puree until smooth.

Warm Endive and Kale Salad

2	tablespoons olive oil		½	head kale (redbor, green, or purple), stems trimmed, leaves chopped
2	cloves garlic, peeled and chopped		2	tablespoons nonalcoholic white wine
1	head Belgian endive, cut in half lengthwise then sliced crosswise		1	tablespoon chopped fresh basil
				Salt and ground black pepper

Heat the oil in a large skillet over medium-high heat. Add the garlic and sauté for about 30 seconds. Add the endive, sauté until lightly browned, about 2 minutes, then add the kale. Add the white wine, stirring occasionally to deglaze the pan (scrape up any browned bits). Cook for about 1 minute more. Off the heat, add the basil and salt and pepper to taste.

To serve, divide the salad among 4 plates, and place 3 quinoa cakes on each. Drizzle some of the horseradish cream sauce on top and spoon some beet caviar around each salad.

Mushroom Walnut Roast

Chef Ken Charney
Monthly Dining Event Chef
Recipe from *The Bold Vegetarian Chef*, published by John Wiley & Sons

Walnuts, tofu and oats make for a familiar yet distinctive taste that resembles a traditional meatloaf. Like meatloaf, this tastes great hot or cold. Serve with mashed potatoes and a vegetable and top with a sauce, like Nutritional Yeast Gravy (page 129) or Roasted Vegetable Sauce (page 140).

Serves 6 to 8

3	tablespoons olive oil	2	tablespoons nonalcoholic red wine or red wine vinegar
1	large onion, chopped fine		
3	cloves garlic, minced	1	tablespoon soy sauce
½	cup coarsely chopped walnuts, toasted	1	tablespoon vegetarian Worcestershire sauce
½	cup rolled oats (regular or quick)		Salt and freshly ground pepper
4	ounces fresh shiitake mushrooms, stems removed, caps thinly sliced	1	package (14 –16 ounces) firm tofu, pressed of excess water, crumbled
2	cups vegetable broth or water	3	tablespoons arrowroot powder
3	tablespoons Dijon mustard	1 –1½	cups dried whole-wheat or white breadcrumbs
2	tablespoons tomato paste		

Preheat the oven to 350°F. Lightly oil a 9 by 5 by 3-inch loaf pan and set aside. In a large nonstick skillet, heat 1½ tablespoons of the oil over medium heat. Add the onion and cook, stirring occasionally, until soft and golden brown, 7 to 10 minutes. Add the garlic and cook until fragrant, 1 to 2 minutes longer. Set aside in large bowl.

In the same skillet, heat the remaining oil over medium heat. Add the walnuts, oats and mushrooms. Sauté for a few minutes, stirring frequently, until the mushrooms are tender. Add a splash of broth or water if the ingredients stick too much.

Stir in a small amount of broth, turn up the heat, and deglaze the pan (scraping the pan bottom to loosen the stuck-on bits of food). Add the remaining broth and cook for 10 minutes. Add the mustard, tomato paste, red wine, soy sauce and Worcestershire sauce. Continue to cook until the mixture is thick, 2 to 3 minutes. Add to the bowl with the onions and set aside. Season generously with salt and pepper to taste.

Place the tofu and arrowroot in a food processor and puree until smooth. Add to the onion mixture and stir in enough breadcrumbs to make a thick paste. Mix well. Pour into the prepared loaf pan. Press down firmly to pack the mixture into the pan.

Bake for 40 minutes. For optimal results, let the loaf cool for 2 hours before slicing it, or make it a day ahead and reheat.

Chef's Tip
For a perfect crispy top, place an additional pan of water in the oven while you bake the loaf.

Reprinted with permission

Vegetarian Grain Meat

Chef David Lee
Presenter at Vegfest
The Field Roast Grain Meat Company
www.fieldroast.com

Chef David Lee specializes in grain meats. This one, with its wonderful spring herb flavor, is one of his favorites. To make this recipe, you'll need cheesecloth, string, and a meat thermometer. Vital wheat gluten is sold in the baking or bulk aisle in natural foods stores.

Serves 2 to 4, sliced thinly

Wet Mix
- 3 tablespoons plus 1 teaspoon olive oil
- 1 tablespoon chopped shallot
- 1 tablespoon chopped carrot
- 1 tablespoon chopped celery
- 1 tablespoon chopped shiitake mushroom
- 2 cloves garlic, minced or pressed through a garlic press
- ¾ cup plus 3 tablespoons water
- 1 teaspoon chopped fresh tarragon
- 1 teaspoon chopped fresh chives
- 1 teaspoon chopped fresh dill
  Juice and grated zest of ½ lemon

Dry Mix
- 1 cup vital wheat gluten
- 2 tablespoons unbleached all-purpose flour
- 1 tablespoon vegetable broth powder
- ¼ teaspoon black pepper
  Dark chili powder for coloring

- 6 quarts water
  Salt

To prepare the wet mix, heat 1 teaspoon of the oil in a small skillet over medium heat, add the shallot, carrot, celery, and mushroom, and sauté 5 minutes. Remove from the heat, add the pressed garlic, stir, and set aside. Combine the water and the remaining 3 tablespoons oil in a medium bowl. Add the tarragon, chives, dill, lemon juice and zest, and the sautéed vegetables to the water and oil, and stir well.

To prepare the dry mix, combine the wheat gluten, flour, vegetable broth powder and pepper in a large bowl. Pour the wet mixture into the dry mixture, and lightly mix by hand for 10 seconds; don't overmix.

With your hands, form the dough into a loaf shape. Cut out a rectangle of cheesecloth 12 inches long and at least 4 inches wider than the length of the loaf, and place it on your work surface with one of the short ends facing you. Place the loaf across the cheesecloth near the end closest to you, and wrap it in the cheesecloth like you would a burrito, folding in the sides before rolling. Secure the cheesecloth with cotton string.

Bring 6 quarts of water to a boil in an 8-quart stockpot. Add salt to taste. Place the wrapped loaf in the boiling water, bring back to a slow boil and cook until the loaf reaches an internal temperature of 190°F, about 1 hour. Cool, remove the cheesecloth and rub the outside of the loaf with dark chili powder for color.

Sloppy Norms

Nearly Normal's
109 NW 15th Street, Corvallis, OR (541) 753-0791

Serve these sandwiches with chips, pickles and coleslaw.

Serves 6

1 package firm tofu (14–16 ounces), crumbled	1 (15-ounce) can tomato sauce
8 ounces tempeh, crumbled	1 tablespoon prepared mustard
¼ cup tamari	1 tablespoon rice syrup or maple syrup
½ cup canola oil	2 tablespoons chili powder
1 large onion, chopped fine	½ teaspoon black pepper
1 large green bell pepper, chopped	¼ teaspoon salt
	6 whole-wheat sandwich buns

Place the tofu and tempeh in a large shallow bowl, add the tamari, stir to coat and set aside.

In a medium saucepan or large skillet, heat ¼ cup of the oil over medium heat and sauté the onion and pepper until tender. Add the tomato sauce, mustard, syrup, chili powder, pepper and salt. Reduce heat to low and simmer for 15 to 20 minutes.

In a separate large skillet, heat the remaining ¼ cup of oil over medium heat. Add the tofu and tempeh and cook, stirring, until browned. Add the sauce and stir well to combine. Serve hot on the sandwich buns.

Happy Spaghetti Sauce

Griggs Irving
Vegetarians of Washington, Seattle, WA

This easy-to-make sauce, with its mystery ingredient (apple), has long been a winner with family and friends. You can use any type of pasta for this dish. I suggest capellini (angel hair), as it cooks in 4 minutes and kids seem to like the really thin strands…Griggs Irving

Serves 4

2	tablespoons canola or safflower oil, plus more if needed
2	apples, cored and diced (with or without skins—your choice)
1	medium onion, chopped
16	ounces firm tofu, cubed
1	(26-ounce) jar of your favorite prepared commercial meatless spaghetti sauce
1	pound of your favorite pasta
	Salt

Put the oil in a large skillet and heat over medium-high heat (add more oil if necessary to coat the entire bottom of the pan) and heat until shimmering. Add the apple cubes and sauté, turning often, until they are golden brown on all sides. Using a slotted spoon, remove the fried apple cubes from the skillet and set aside, leaving the oil in the pan.

Add the chopped onion to the skillet and fry until wilted and just beginning to brown. Reduce the heat to medium-low, add the spaghetti sauce, tofu cubes and apples, and cook until all the ingredients are heated through.

While the sauce is cooking, bring 4 quarts of water to a boil in a large pot, and salt it generously. Prepare the pasta according to package directions.

Chef's Tip
To get every last bit of spaghetti sauce from the "empty" jar, Griggs suggests pouring a splash of already opened nonalcoholic wine (white or red) into the jar. Slosh it around, then pour the wine and sauce into the pan. This gives a subtle improvement to the sauce. You can also use water or fruit juice.

Soul-Full Chili

Chef Dreena Burton
Author, Presenter at Vegfest
Recipe from *The Everyday Vegan,* published by Arsenal Pulp Press
www.everydayvegan.com

This is a thick, hearty, stick-to-your-ribs stew. Feel free to choose ingredients that have extra layers of flavor built in; spicy or garlic-flavored tomato paste adds zip, while fire-roasted canned tomatoes and chipotle-flavored hot sauce lend a smoky element. Canned beans work well in this recipe, and you can substitute other kinds if you like, or use just one kind instead of two.

Serves 8 to 10

1 tablespoon olive oil	1 pound red, green, or yellow bell peppers, or a combination, chopped (about 2½ cups)
2 large red onions, chopped (about 2½ cups)	
3 ribs celery, chopped	2 cups frozen corn kernels (or fresh corn cut from the cob)
2 medium carrots, chopped fine	
8–10 medium cloves garlic, minced	1 cup cooked kidney beans
1 tablespoon chili powder	1 cup cooked black beans
1 teaspoon dried oregano	2 (28-ounce) cans diced tomatoes
¾ teaspoon ground cumin	1 (5½-ounce) can tomato paste
⅛ teaspoon ground cinnamon	½ teaspoon hot sauce
⅛ teaspoon red pepper flakes (optional)	1 tablespoon dark soy sauce or tamari
Sea salt	1 teaspoon sugar
Freshly ground black pepper	

Heat the oil in a large stockpot or Dutch oven over medium heat, add the onions, cover, and sauté for 2 to 3 minutes (lift cover and stir occasionally). Add the celery and carrots, cook covered for another 2 to 3 minutes, then add the garlic, chili powder, oregano, cumin, cinnamon, red pepper flakes if using, ½ teaspoon salt, and pepper to taste. Stir and cook for 3 to 4 minutes. (If the ingredients are dry, add a few tablespoons of water.) Add the peppers and corn, and cook another 3 to 4 minutes (cover and stir). Add the beans, diced tomatoes with their juice, tomato paste, hot sauce, soy sauce and sugar. Turn the heat to high and let the chili come to a boil. Reduce the heat to low and simmer, covered, for 20 minutes. Adjust the seasonings and serve.

Dirty Rice *Cajun*

The LocoMotive
291 E 5th Street, Eugene, OR (541) 465-4754
www.thelocomotive.com

At the LocoMotive, guests receive a little bowl of this extremely popular rice dish with some bread as an amuse-bouche (appetizer) when they arrive. However, served in more substantial portions it makes a wonderful side dish or even main course. It's an often-requested recipe.

Serves 8 as a side dish

4   cups cooked, drained, unseasoned black-eyed peas (or any other legume of choice)
2   cups cooked white rice
    Salt and ground black pepper
½   cup olive oil

4   scallions, white and green parts, chopped (about 1cup)
5   Roma tomatoes, cut into ¼-inch dice (about 2 cups)
1   tablespoon plus ½ teaspoon Tabasco sauce (or to taste)

In a large bowl, mix the black-eyed peas, rice, 1½ teaspoons salt, ½ teaspoon black pepper and olive oil thoroughly. Add the scallions, tomatoes and Tabasco sauce and re-mix. Taste and correct the seasonings. If the acidity is insufficient, add more Tabasco; the mixture should be a little tart. Refrigerate. If serving several hours later, taste again; this usually requires some extra salt (about ¼ teaspoon) and maybe extra Tabasco to compensate for what soaks into the beans and rice over time. Serve chilled or at room temperature.

Pecan Fried Wild Rice

Chef Dreena Burton

Author, Presenter at Vegfest
Recipe from *Vive le Vegan!,* published by Arsenal Pulp Press
www.everydayvegan.com

This dish is simple and very flavorful. It's also surprisingly fast to prepare, and you'll save even more time by cooking the rice a day or two in advance.

Serves 4 to 5 as a side dish

1½ tablespoons extra-virgin olive oil	½ cup chopped pecans, toasted in a dry skillet until fragrant
4–4½ cups cooked wild rice/brown rice mixture *(see Chef's Tip)*	2 tablespoons tamari
Freshly ground black pepper	1 teaspoon toasted sesame oil
½ cup frozen green peas	Sea salt
5 scallions, chopped	

Heat the oil in a skillet over medium heat. When the oil is hot, add the cooked rice, season with pepper to taste, and sauté for 2 to 3 minutes, stirring occasionally. Add the frozen peas and cook, stirring, for another 2 to 3 minutes, then add the scallions, pecans, and tamari. Stir until the peas are heated through and the green scallions have wilted and cooked a little, about 3 minutes. Turn off the heat, stir in the tamari and sesame oil, and season to taste with sea salt and pepper if desired.

Chef's Tip

You can use all wild or all brown rice, or a wild and brown rice mix for this dish. Wild rice is particularly nice to use because it adds an earthy flavor that works well with the other ingredients. Dreena uses roughly ¾ cup each of wild rice and brown basmati rice. Rinse the rice, and combine with close to 4 cups of water and a few pinches of sea salt in a saucepan. Bring to a boil, stir through, then reduce heat to low and cover. Let simmer until the water is absorbed and the wild rice is tender and has opened up, 45 to 50 minutes. Let cool a little, or refrigerate until ready to use. If you use more wild rice, you will need more water.

Broccoli and Cashews over Millet

Debra Wasserman
Author, Co-director of the Vegetarian Resource Group
Recipe from *Simply Vegan,* published by the Vegetarian Resource Group
www.vrg.org

Light and delicate, millet is a nice, high-protein alternative to couscous. The combination of millet, cashews, and broccoli makes a substantial side dish.

Serves 5

2	cups millet
6½	cups water
2	tablespoons oil
2	teaspoons mustard seed
1	large bunch broccoli, chopped
1	medium onion, chopped
½	cup cashews, chopped
1	tablespoon soy sauce

Place the millet and 6 cups of the water in a medium saucepan, cover and cook over medium-high heat until the millet is soft, 15 to 20 minutes. While the millet is cooking, heat the oil in a large pan. Add the mustard seeds and cover the pan. As the seeds fry they will begin to pop (like popcorn). When you no longer hear any seeds popping (a minute or so), add the broccoli, onion, the remaining ½ cup water, cashews and soy sauce. Sauté the ingredients until the broccoli is tender, about 15 minutes. Serve the sautéed mixture over the cooked millet.

Reprinted with permission

Tasty Beet Goodness

Swan Café

1220 N Forest, Bellingham, WA (360) 734-8158
www.communityfood.coop

This dish is good warm or cold, as a side dish or salad. Since you'll be steaming the beets whole, try to find beets that are all the same size so they'll cook evenly.

Serves 6

2½ pounds red beets, scrubbed	1 bunch green chard, stemmed and chopped
1½ pounds golden beets with greens, beets scrubbed and greens cleaned and chopped	⅓ cup lemon juice
2 tablespoons canola oil	1 teaspoon chili powder
2 tablespoons olive oil	1 teaspoon sea salt
1½ cups red onion, chopped	

Place all the beets in a steamer basket set in a large saucepan over an inch of water, cover, and steam until tender, 30 to 45 minutes. Cool slightly and peel off the skins, keeping the colors separated. Cut the red beets in slices and the golden beets in chunks, and place in a large bowl. Heat the oils in a large skillet over medium heat, add the onions, and sauté until softened, 2 to 3 minutes. Add the beet greens and chard and sauté until wilted and soft, about 2 minutes more. Add the cooked greens and onions to the beets, sprinkle the lemon juice, chili powder and salt over the vegetables, and toss very gently. Serve.

Nutritional Yeast Gravy

Keystone Café
395 W 5th Avenue, Eugene, OR (541) 342-2075

This is a versatile gravy that can be used as sauce over rice, veggies, or potatoes, or in shepherd's pie. All it takes is your imagination. It's quick and easy to prepare. One warning: it is habit-forming—just ask some of our customers! Spoon this over the Vegetarian Grain Meat recipe on page 120.

Makes 2 quarts

1	red or green bell pepper, chopped
1	medium onion, chopped
2	quarts water
¼	cup soy sauce
1	cup canola oil
1¼	cup organic white flour
¾	cup nutritional yeast flakes

Blanch the pepper and the onion by adding them to a pot of rapidly boiling water and cooking for 1 minute. Drain through a colander and set aside.

Bring the water and soy sauce to a boil in a medium saucepan and keep at a simmer. Meanwhile, in another medium saucepan, heat the oil over medium-high heat. Make a roux by whisking the flour slowly into the oil; cook, stirring constantly, for about 5 minutes. Add the nutritional yeast flakes. Remove the water/soy sauce mixture from the heat and add to the roux, stirring constantly. The gravy will thicken right away. Add the blanched pepper and onion to the gravy and stir.

Tamale Pie

Chef Louise Hagler

Presenter at Vegfest
Recipe from *The New Farm Vegetarian Cookbook,* published by The Book Publishing Company

This savory casserole is a great do-ahead dish, simply wrap tightly and refrigerate until ready to use. Add 5 or 10 minutes to the baking time; the mixture should be bubbling.

Serves 4

1 cup yellow cornmeal	2 cups diced tomatoes, fresh or canned
1 cup cold water	1 tablespoon chili powder
3 cups boiling water	2 teaspoons cumin
2 tablespoons oil	1 teaspoon oregano
1 medium onion, chopped	1 teaspoon salt
1 large green bell pepper, chopped	½ teaspoon garlic powder
1 jalapeño pepper, minced (optional)	2 cups cooked pinto beans

Combine the cornmeal and cold water in a medium bowl to make a mush. Pour the boiling water into the mush, whisking to keep smooth. Place in the top section of a double boiler, cover, and cook for 25 minutes, whisking occasionally.

Preheat the oven to 350°F. Heat the oil in a medium saucepan over medium heat and add the onion, green pepper, and jalapeño pepper, if using. Sauté until the vegetables are softened, about 10 minutes. Add the tomatoes, chili powder, cumin, oregano, salt and garlic powder, stir, and cook to heat through.

Spread half the mush in a small casserole dish or 7 by 11-inch baking pan. Spread the beans evenly over the mush, then cover with the tomato mixture. Spread the remaining cornmeal mush on top. Bake until the surface is golden brown and the casserole is bubbling around the edges, about 30 minutes.

Reprinted with permission

Brazilian Black Beans

Chef Dawn Hainey
Culinary Instructor, Arlington, WA
Recipe from *Taste and See,* published by Cooks by Morris Press

Although canned beans are convenient, there's something very satisfying about cooking your own "from scratch." For the best results, buy from a store with a high turnover; the beans should be shiny and firm, not wrinkled. These beans need to be started a few hours ahead of when you will be eating them, or you can start the cooking process the night before.

Serves 4

8 ounces black beans, picked over and rinsed	3 cups water
½ cup chopped onion	1 cup white or brown rice
2 cloves garlic, minced	1 medium sweet potato, peeled, halved and sliced ¼ inch thick
1 bay leaf	1 (14½-ounce) can diced tomatoes
6 tablespoons minced fresh parsley	½ teaspoon minced orange zest
½ teaspoon salt	

Place the beans in a large saucepan, and add enough water to cover them. Bring to a boil, reduce the heat and simmer for 2 minutes. Remove the pan from the heat, cover and let stand for 1 hour. Alternatively, you can place the beans in water to cover in a large saucepan, cover and set in a cool place for 6 to 8 hours or overnight.

Drain the beans in a colander and rinse them, then return the beans to the saucepan. Add the onion, garlic, bay leaf, 4 tablespoons of the parsley, and the salt. Pour in the water and stir. Bring to a boil, reduce the heat, cover and simmer until the beans are tender, about 1½ hours, adding more water if necessary and stirring occasionally. Meanwhile, cook the rice according to the package directions. In a small saucepan, bring 4 cups of water to a boil, add the sweet potato, and cook until tender, 15 to 20 minutes. Drain.

Remove the bay leaf from the beans and discard. Add the tomatoes to the bean mixture. Uncover and simmer, stirring occasionally, until a thick gravy forms, about 10 minutes. Stir in the orange peel. To serve, spoon some of the hot rice onto each plate, spoon the beans over the rice, sprinkle the remaining parsley over the beans, and place a few slices of sweet potato on the side.

Yam Enchiladas

Oceana Natural Foods Cooperative
159 SE 2nd Street, Newport, OR (541) 265-3893
www.oceanafoods.org

Yams are used often in cooking in Central and South America. They can grow quite large and may be sold in chunks in Latin American markets. What we call "yams" in this country are in fact a dark-fleshed variety of sweet potato. Although they're not related to true yams, sweet potatoes make an acceptable substitute in recipes like this one.

Serves 6 to 8

Sauce

2   tablespoons olive oil
2   medium yellow onions, diced
5   cloves garlic, minced
¼   cup sweet paprika
1   tablespoon ground cumin
1   tablespoon whole coriander
1   tablespoon chili powder
1½   teaspoons sea salt
1   bay leaf
6   tablespoons brown rice flour
4½   cups tomato sauce, homemade or commercially prepared

Filling

1½   pounds yam, peeled and sliced into ¼-inch-thick slices (about 4½ cups)
2   cloves garlic, minced
1½   teaspoons cumin
1   tablespoon olive oil
15 –18   small white corn tortillas
3   cups shredded almond or soy cheese
¾   cup diced scallions
6   tablespoons chopped black olives
6   tablespoons diced green chiles
¾   cup soy sour cream
Chopped fresh cilantro

Heat the oven to 400°F. For the sauce, heat the oil in a large skillet over medium heat, add the onions and sauté until they are translucent, about 5 minutes. Add the paprika, cumin, coriander, chili powder, salt and bay leaf, stir to blend, and cook for 5 more minutes. Add the rice flour and the tomato sauce and whisk thoroughly. Reduce heat to low and simmer for at least 10 minutes.

For the filling, toss the yam slices with the cumin, garlic and olive oil. Bake on a baking sheet until soft, about 30 minutes. Remove the yam slices and reduce the oven heat to 350°F. To assemble, pour one third of the sauce in the bottom of a 9 by 13-inch casserole and add one layer of tortillas. Spread half of the yams evenly in the pan, then sprinkle in half of the shredded almond or soy cheese, and half the diced scallions, olives and green chiles. Pour more sauce on top. Add another layer of tortillas, top with the rest of the yams, the rest of the scallions, olives, and green chiles, and cover with the remaining sauce. Sprinkle the remaining cheese evenly over the top.

Cover and bake for one hour, then uncover and bake until the top is browned, 5 to 10 minutes longer. Cut and serve garnished with the chopped cilantro.

Tacos de Chayote

Agua Verde Paddle Club
1303 NE Boat Street, Seattle, WA (206) 545-8570
www.aguaverde.com

Epazote is a pungent herb, available dried in Latin markets. It's often added to bean dishes as much for its carminative (gas-reducing) properties as for its unique flavor. Chayote (pronounced chi-OH-tay) is a mild, pale green squash about the size of a pear. If you like, accompany this dish with Pineapple Jicama Salsa, page 60.

Serves 4

12	small corn tortillas	3	medium zucchini, cubed
1	medium onion, diced	3	chayotes, seeded and cubed
3	cloves garlic, minced	½	cup raisins
1	tablespoon dried epazote		Minced fresh cilantro
3	tablespoons olive oil		
1	(28-ounce) can whole tomatoes, drained and chopped		

Heat the tortillas on a hot griddle to soften them, then wrap them in foil to keep warm and set them aside. In a medium bowl, combine the onion, garlic, epazote, 2 tablespoons of the olive oil, and the tomatoes, and set aside. Heat the remaining tablespoon of oil in a large skillet over medium heat and add the zucchini, chayotes and raisins. Sauté until the squash is just crisp-tender. Add the tomato mixture and sauté until heated through, being careful not to overcook the squash. It should have a slight crunch. Spoon the filling onto the warmed tortillas and sprinkle with the cilantro.

Tempeh Tacos

Rita Condon, BS Nutrition
PCC Cooks Culinary Instructor
www.pccnaturalmarkets.com/pcccooks/instructors

This is an ideal "do it yourself" meal. Serve the taco shells, filling, and condiments family-style at the table and let everyone build their own protein-rich tempeh tacos.

Serves 4

1	tablespoon extra virgin olive oil
1	large onion, diced
5	large cloves garlic, minced fine
	Salt
4½	teaspoons ground cumin
1	tablespoon chili powder (or to taste)
2	(8-ounce) packages tempeh, chopped fine
1	(6-ounce) can tomato paste
1	package taco shells

Taco Condiments

1	cup shredded cheddar-style soy cheese
2	medium tomatoes, chopped fine
3	ounces sprouts, such as alfalfa, broccoli, or radish
1	ripe avocado, chopped
	Taco sauce or salsa

Put the olive oil in a large skillet and warm over medium heat. Add the diced onions, garlic and about 1½ teaspoons salt. Sauté until the onions begin to soften and turn translucent, about 5 minutes. Add the cumin and chili powder and stir to incorporate. Add the tempeh, stir to incorporate and sauté for 5 minutes, stirring regularly so the mixture doesn't stick to the bottom of the skillet. Add the tomato paste and 1½ cups water. Stir until all the tomato paste and water are thoroughly blended with the tempeh mixture. The mixture should be thick but not dry. If it is dry, add up to 6 tablespoons water. Taste and add salt and extra spices if necessary. Cover the skillet, reduce heat to low and cook for 10 minutes.

Place some tempeh taco filling in the bottom of each taco shell. Top with shredded soy cheese, tomatoes, avocado and sprouts. Sprinkle taco sauce over the top.

Quinoa with Cumin and Lime

Olympia Food Coop
3111 Pacific Avenue SE, Olympia, WA (360) 956-3870

This is especially good with fresh squeezed lime juice. It is very fast and easy to put together; you can prepare all the other ingredients while the quinoa cooks. This recipe will convert people who think they don't like quinoa.

Serves 8

2 cups quinoa, rinsed well	¼ cup golden raisins
⅓ cup lime juice	¼ cup currants
⅓ cup canola oil	1 red onion, thinly sliced
1 tablespoon garlic, minced	¼ cup pine nuts, toasted
2 teaspoons cumin	1 small bunch cilantro, minced
2 teaspoons salt	
1 jalapeño pepper, seeded and minced	

In a large saucepan, bring 6 cups of water to a boil over high heat. Add the quinoa and cook until done, 10 to 15 minutes. It is done when the grains are almost completely translucent, with just a small opaque dot in the center. Do not overcook.

Meanwhile, make the dressing: In a medium bowl, whisk together the lime juice, canola oil, garlic, cumin, jalapeño and salt.

Drain the quinoa into a colander (make sure that the holes are small enough so that the quinoa doesn't escape) and rinse with cold water. Drain thoroughly. Place the quinoa in a bowl and pour the dressing over it. Add the golden raisins and currants, mix together and refrigerate until completely cool.

When the quinoa is cold, add the onion, pine nuts and cilantro. Mix well and serve.

Spicy Chipotle Marinade

Berry Fields Café
201 S Pearl Street, Centralia, WA (360) 736-1183

This easy, zesty marinade is great for grilling fresh veggies or as a marinade for tofu.

Makes 1½ cups

½	cup olive oil
¼	cup minced garlic
½	cup fresh orange juice
½	cup fresh lime juice
¼	cup Tabasco chipotle sauce
1	teaspoon salt
1	teaspoon ground cumin

Heat the oil in a small saucepan over medium heat. Stir in the garlic and cook 15 seconds, until the garlic releases its fragrance. Remove from the heat, cool slightly, then stir in the remaining ingredients, return to the heat and bring to a boil. Remove from the heat and cool.

Columbian Café Summer Pasta Italian

Columbian Café

1114 Marine Drive, Astoria, OR (503) 325 2233

This pasta dish is simplicity itself, allowing the vibrant flavors of the ingredients to really come through. Why not splurge on a gourmet brand of pasta to try with this?

Serves 2

8	ounces fresh or dried pasta
1	medium onion, chopped
	Extra virgin olive oil
8	cloves garlic minced
2	tablespoons pine nuts
4 or 5	Roma tomatoes, chopped
1	bunch fresh basil, chopped or chiffonade *(see below)*

Cook the pasta according to package directions or to taste. Heat the olive oil in a medium skillet over medium heat. Add the onion and sauté for about 2 minutes, then add the garlic and continue to sauté until the onions turn translucent. Add the pine nuts and cook for another 2 minutes. Add the tomatoes and cook just until hot through. Remove from the heat, add the basil and immediately toss with pasta.

Chiffonade

Chiffonade is a French term (literally "made of rags") that refers to thin strips or shreds of leafy vegetables or herbs, such as lettuce, spinach, or basil. These lacy strips are used to garnish soups, salads, and other dishes. To create basil chiffonade, remove the stems, make a stack of the leaves, and roll them tightly. Holding the roll with your fingers, slice it crosswise into thin strips.

Portobello Mushroom Penne *Italian*

California Pizza Kitchen
401 Northgate Way, Seattle, WA (206) 367-4445

For a number of years now, Americans have had a love affair with the big, meaty-tasting mushrooms known as portobellos, and the passion shows no signs of decreasing. This rapidly prepared pasta dish captures the steak-like mushroom's appeal, combining it with other varieties that have become widely available in well-stocked supermarkets, greengrocers, and farmers' markets. If you can't find one or more of the mushrooms, feel free to substitute equal quantities of others that you like…California Pizza Kitchen

Serves 4 to 6

¼ cup olive oil (not extra virgin)	Salt
8 ounces portobello mushrooms, sliced ¼ inch thick	3½ tablespoons chopped fresh thyme
8 ounces white mushrooms, sliced ¼ inch thick	1 pound dry penne pasta
4 ounces shiitake mushrooms, sliced ⅛ inch thick	¼ cup extra-virgin olive oil
4 ounces oyster mushrooms, sliced ⅛ inch thick	4 tablespoons minced garlic (about 12 cloves)
4 ounces cremini mushrooms, sliced ⅛ inch thick	1 tablespoon chopped fresh Italian parsley

In a large nonstick frying pan, heat the olive oil over high heat. Add the portobello and white mushrooms and cook, stirring frequently, for 5 minutes. Add the remaining mushrooms and thyme, salt to taste, and continue to cook, stirring frequently, until the mushrooms are lightly browned, 5 to 7 minutes more. Remove them from the heat and set aside.

Bring a large pot of salted water to a rapid boil. Add the pasta and cook until al dente, 8 to 9 minutes. Meanwhile, in a large nonstick frying pan, heat the extra virgin olive oil over medium-high heat. Add the garlic and salt to taste and cook, stirring, for 1 minute. Stir in the portobello mushroom mixture, thyme and parsley. Cook, stirring, for 2 minutes.

Drain the pasta thoroughly and toss it with the mushrooms in a large mixing or serving bowl until the pasta is well coated with the mushroom mixture. Serve.

Roasted Vegetable Sauce for Pasta Italian

The LocoMotive

291 E 5th Street, Eugene, OR (541) 465-4754
www.thelocomotive.com

One of the LocoMotive's most popular seasonal pasta sauces, this is also good added to soups or vegetable stews, or served as a spread or dip. Refrigerated, it keeps well for at least a month. Adjust the number and type of chiles to your taste. For a mild sauce, omit the jalapeños and Anaheims and add an extra small red or green bell pepper. For a very hot version, substitute fresh cayennes for the jalapeños and use more chiles than specified.

Makes about 5 cups (serves 8 to 10)

1 large red onion, peeled and halved	1 large Anaheim chile (red, if available)
4 large ripe, red tomatoes, cored	1 large red bell pepper
1 head of garlic, left whole, outer layers of paper removed, tops of cloves trimmed off	½ cup packed basil leaves, plus more for garnish
Olive oil for pan and vegetables, plus 1 tablespoon for sautéing basil	3 tablespoons nonalcoholic red wine
	2½–3 teaspoons salt
1 medium jalapeño chile	½ teaspoon black pepper
	Grated zest of 1 lemon

Preheat the oven to 450°F. Line a roasting pan with foil (for easy cleanup) and then coat it with olive oil. Oil the onions, tomatoes, garlic, chiles and red pepper with your hands and place them in the oiled pan. Roast until the vegetables are soft and browned in places, and the peppers are collapsed (about 1 hour), turning and rearranging the vegetables every 10 to 15 minutes for even cooking.

Meanwhile, coarsely chop the basil and sauté it in olive oil on medium-low heat just until very aromatic, 2 to 3 minutes.

When the vegetables are cooked, remove the cores from the chiles, and the cores and seeds from the red peppers. Working in batches if necessary, reduce all the roasted vegetables (with all the accumulated pan juice) and the sautéed basil to a coarse puree in a food processor, blender or food mill.

In a pot of adequate size, bring the puree to a boil. Reduce it to a simmer, add the wine, most of the salt and pepper, and cook uncovered for about 5 minutes. Taste and adjust the seasonings, adding the remaining salt if desired.

Toss with freshly cooked pasta or serve plain pasta into bowls and put a large dollop of sauce in the center of each serving so people can toss their own. Garnish with lemon zest or gratings over the pasta and fresh basil leaves on the side of the dish, if desired.

Wild Mushroom Risotto *Italian*

Ellen Purington
Magnolia Vegetarian Cooking Club, Seattle, WA

For the best flavor, make sure that the mushrooms you use include some shiitake mushrooms. Look for packaged dried mushrooms labeled "forest" or "mixed wild mushrooms." Mushroom broth enhances the mushroom flavor in the dish, but this recipe also works well with any vegetable broth.

Serves 6

8	dried mushrooms
4	cups mushroom or vegetable broth
2	tablespoons olive oil
1	medium sweet onion, chopped fine
1½	cups Arborio rice, rinsed and drained well
½	cup dry nonalcoholic white wine, optional (If you use wine reduce the broth by ½ cup.)
¼–½	cup chopped Italian parsley
1	cup grated Parmesan-style nondairy cheese

Soak the dried mushroom in lukewarm water until soft, approximately 20 minutes. Remove and squeeze out excess water. Cut the mushrooms into very thin strips. Set aside. Heat the vegetable broth and pour it into a heatproof liquid measuring cup.

Heat the olive oil in a large saucepan over medium heat. Add the onion and cook, stirring, until translucent but not brown, about 10 minutes. Add the rice to the saucepan. Cook for 2 minutes, stirring gently but continuously. Add the wine, if using, and stir another few minutes. Add the broth, ½ cup at a time, to the rice, stirring constantly until the broth is completely absorbed. Repeat this up until the last ½ cup of broth is added. All of the liquid must be absorbed before you add the next ½ cup of broth to the saucepan. The constant stirring helps the rice to cook evenly and keeps the mixture from burning or clumping up. With the last ½ cup of broth, add the mushrooms. Again, stir constantly until the broth is completely absorbed.

Add the Italian Parsley and cheese. Mix thoroughly. When you're ready to serve, place the risotto into a serving dish and garnish with a light dusting of grated cheese and a few sprigs of parsley.

Toby's Tofu Piccata *Italian*

Chef Toby Alves
Presenter at Vegfest
Toby's Tofu Palace
www.tofupalace.com

Tofu speaks Italian in this easy entrée. Broccoli rabe would make a nice accompaniment to this dish. It was presented at Vegfest.

Serves 4

6 tablespoons lemon juice	Italian seasoning
2 tablespoons soy sauce	¼ cup olive oil
3 tablespoons minced garlic	⅓ cup nonalcoholic white wine
16 ounces firm tofu, blotted dry, sliced ¼-inch thick	¼ cup nonhydrogenated margarine, softened
2 tablespoons unbleached flour	¼ cup capers, drained
2 tablespoons corn meal	
Salt and ground black pepper	

In a large shallow bowl, whisk together 2 tablespoons of the lemon juice, the soy sauce, and 1 tablespoon of the minced garlic. Add the tofu slices to this mixture and marinate for 1 hour.

Combine the flour, corn meal, salt and pepper to taste, and Italian seasoning and pour into a large, shallow dish. Line a large plate with paper towels. Heat 3 tablespoons of the olive oil in a large nonstick skillet over medium-high heat. Dip the tofu slices in the breading mixture and sauté until golden, about 2 minutes on each side. Remove the cooked tofu from the skillet and place on the paper-towel-lined plate.

Wipe out the skillet, return it to the heat, and add the remaining tablespoon of oil. Sauté the remaining 2 tablespoons of garlic, being careful not to burn it. Add the remaining 4 tablespoons of lemon juice, the wine, and half the margarine, stir well, and add the tofu to the pan. Simmer until the liquid is reduced by half. Whisk in the remaining margarine and the capers. Season to taste with salt and pepper. Serve hot.

Seitan à la Bourguignonne French

Chef Ken Charney

Monthly Dining Event Chef
Recipe from *The Bold Vegetarian Chef*, published by John Wiley & Sons

With no apologies to Bœuf à la Bourguignonne, here is a version of the French stew cooked in red wine. This vegetarian version is incredibly rich, slightly sweet and very satisfying. Serve over rice or noodles.

Serves 4 to 6

¼ cup unbleached all-purpose flour
1 (8-ounce) package seitan, cut in bite-size chunks
3 tablespoons olive oil, plus more if necessary
1 onion, sliced thin
1 leek (white and tender green parts), sliced into half-moons
12 ounces cremini or Portobello mushrooms (or a combination), sliced thin
1 tablespoon minced fresh thyme
2 teaspoons minced fresh rosemary

2 carrots, cut into bite-size chunks
3 cloves garlic, sliced thin
1 teaspoon salt
¼ teaspoon freshly ground pepper
2 cups nonalcoholic red wine
3 tablespoons tomato paste
1 bay leaf
1 cup vegetable broth
2 tablespoons balsamic vinegar
2–3 tablespoons coarsely chopped fresh parsley
1 tablespoon fresh lemon juice

Place the flour in a sealable plastic bag. Add the seitan and shake until all the pieces are well coated. Put the coated seitan on a plate and set aside.

In a Dutch oven or large soup pot, heat 2 tablespoons of the olive oil over medium-high heat. Fry the seitan in batches without crowding until browned on all sides. Use tongs to turn the pieces. You may have to add more oil as you go along. Remove the seitan and set aside.

Heat the remaining tablespoon oil in the same pot. Add the onion and leek and cook over medium heat until very soft and lightly browned, 5 to 7 minutes. Add the mushrooms, thyme and rosemary and cook, stirring often, until the mushrooms are tender, about 3 minutes. Add the carrots and garlic and cook for another minute. Season with the salt and pepper.

Add the wine and bring to a boil. Cook for 10 minutes, stirring frequently. Stir in the tomato paste and add the bay leaf. Reduce the heat to a simmer, cover with the lid ajar, and cook for 45 minutes.

Stir in the broth and vinegar. Continue to simmer uncovered for about 15 minutes longer, stirring often, until the stew is thickened to your liking. Stir in the parsley and lemon juice and season with additional salt and pepper to taste.

Reprinted with permission

Tofu Cutlets with Tapenade Sauce *Spanish*

Chef Robin Robertson

Author, Presenter at Vegfest
Recipe from *366 Healthful Ways to Cook Tofu,* published by Penguin
www.robinrobertson.com

The neutral flavor of tofu provides the perfect vehicle for the piquant flavors of the tapenade sauce.

Serves 4

2	tablespoons capers
6	oil-cured olives, pitted
3	oil-packed sun-dried tomatoes, cut into pieces
¼	cup firmly packed fresh parsley leaves
2	tablespoons fresh lemon juice
¼	cup plus 2 tablespoons olive oil
1	package firm tofu (14–16 ounces), cut into eight ½-inch slices

In a food processor, pulse the capers, olives, tomatoes, parsley and lemon juice until the mixture is chopped fine. With the motor running, add ¼ cup of the olive oil in a stream and blend the tapenade sauce until emulsified. Heat the remaining 2 tablespoons olive oil in a large skillet over medium-high heat and cook the tofu until golden brown, about 2 minutes for each side. Serve the tofu topped with the tapenade sauce.

Hungarian Goulash

Chef Julia Terry
Author, Federal Way, WA
Recipe from *Conscious Vegetarian*, published by Julia Terry

Goulash can be served over grains or beans, but this thick stew is substantial enough to eat on its own.

Serves 10

2   tablespoons soybean oil
2   pounds seitan or tempeh, diced
3   medium onions, chopped
2   tablespoons paprika
2   bay leaves
1   teaspoon caraway seeds

1   clove garlic, minced
3   cups water
4   medium potatoes, diced
3   tablespoons tomato paste
½   cup nonalcoholic red wine
    Salt and ground black pepper

Heat the oil in a large saucepan over medium heat. Add the seitan and sauté until lightly browned on all sides. Add the onions and continue to cook until translucent. Add the paprika, bay leaves, caraway seeds, garlic and water. Bring to a boil, cover, and simmer over low heat for 10 minutes. Add the potatoes and simmer for 10 more minutes. Stir in the tomato paste and wine and bring to a boil. Turn the heat off and add salt and pepper to taste. Remove the bay leaf and serve.

Reprinted with permission

Tempeh and Red Pepper Stroganoff *Russian*

Chef Cynthia Lair

Presenter at Vegfest
Nutrition faculty member at Bastyr University
Recipe from *Feeding the Whole Family,* published by Moon Smile Press
www.feedingfamily.com

This mouth-watering tempeh recipe is quick to make and is a beautifully balanced meal served over quinoa, whole-wheat couscous or udon noodles next to a salad of wild greens.

Serves 4

1½ cups soymilk or water	½ teaspoon dried thyme
¼ cup nonalcoholic mirin (Japanese rice wine)	1 large carrot, cut into short, thin strips
3 tablespoons tamari or shoyu (Japanese soy sauce)	1 red bell pepper, cut into thin strips
1 tablespoon extra-virgin olive oil	1 (8-ounce) package tempeh, cut crosswise into ¼-inch strips
1 large onion, chopped	3 tablespoons whole-wheat pastry flour
1–2 cloves garlic, minced	Freshly ground black pepper
½ teaspoon dried oregano	½ cup chopped fresh parsley

In a small bowl, mix the soymilk, mirin and tamari. Heat the oil in a large skillet over medium heat. Add the onion, garlic, oregano and thyme. Sauté until the onions soften. Add the carrots, then the red pepper, then the tempeh, letting each cook for a few minutes before adding the next. When the tempeh starts to become golden, add the flour. Stir it in, coating the ingredients well. Add the soymilk mixture slowly, stirring as you go to make a nice gravy. Season with black pepper to taste. Reduce heat to low and simmer for 10 to 15 minutes. Garnish with the parsley and serve.

Chef's Tip

If you have a little extra time you can bake this dish as a casserole for deeper flavor. Preheat the oven to 300°F, then follow the directions for sautéing the vegetables and tempeh. After you add the black pepper to taste, spoon all the ingredients into a small casserole dish, cover, and bake for 30 minutes. Garnish and serve as above.

Southern Italian Vegetable Stew *Ciambotta*

Chef Bryanna Clark Grogan

Author, Presenter at Vegfest
Recipe from *Nonna's Italian Kitchen,* published by the Book Publishing Company
www.bryannaclarkgrogan.com

This is delicious—deceptively so because the ingredients are so simple. You can vary the vegetables and amounts according to what's in your garden or market. Instead of zucchini, try yellow summer squash, cauliflower or fennel. Serve with a good crusty bread to sop up the good juices.

Serves 4

½ pound eggplant, unpeeled, cut into 1-inch cubes
   Salt
1 tablespoon extra-virgin olive oil
1 large onion, thinly sliced
1 rib celery, thinly sliced
5 large cloves garlic, minced
1 cup fresh basil leaves, chopped
1 pound ripe plum tomatoes, passed through a manual food mill, or peeled and chopped fine in the food processor, or 1 (14-ounce) can plum tomatoes, drained and processed

12 ounces new potatoes, or any waxy potato, scrubbed and cut into large cubes
1 medium zucchini, cut crosswise into ½-inch slices
1 large or 2 small red or yellow bell peppers, and cut into ½-inch strips
2½ teaspoons salt
   Freshly ground black pepper

Toss the eggplant cubes in a colander with 2 teaspoons salt. Place in the sink to drain for 30 minutes. Rinse, drain and pat dry, squeezing a little.

In a large saucepan, heat the oil over medium-high heat. Add the onion, celery and garlic. Stir-cook for about 5 minutes, adding a little water as necessary to prevent sticking and burning. Add the basil and stir-cook for 2 to 3 minutes, then add the tomatoes and bring to a simmer. Add the eggplant, potatoes, and ½ teaspoon salt. Stir, bring to a boil, then reduce heat and simmer, covered, for 15 minutes. Add the zucchini and peppers and simmer until all the vegetables are tender, about 15 minutes. Add salt and pepper to taste, transfer to a warm serving bowl, let stand for 15 minutes and serve.

Shepherd's Pie British

Chef Birgitte Antonsen
Presenter at Vegfest
PCC Cooks Culinary Instructor
www.natureswayfood.com

This shepherd's pie, presented at Vegfest, is topped with mashed root vegetables, instead of the traditional mashed potatoes. The stew in this recipe can be made ahead of time, even frozen and defrosted before use. Herbes de Provence is a blend of dried herbs including basil, lavender, rosemary, and thyme, often sold in small clay crocks. You'll need a total of 1 pound of lentils for this dish; experiment with your own mix or use the proportions suggested in the ingredient list. Serve Shepherd's Pie with broccoli, sautéed kale or other seasonal vegetables.

Serves 6

Lentil Filling
1 tablespoon extra virgin olive oil
2½ medium onions (about 1 pound), diced fine
2 cloves garlic, minced
4 teaspoons Herbes de Provence
2 teaspoons dried basil
1½ teaspoons curry powder
2 bay leaves
¾ cup yellow split peas, picked over and rinsed
¾ cup green lentils, picked over and rinsed
¾ cup French lentils, picked over and rinsed
1 (28-ounce) can tomato puree
4 cups vegetable broth
3 medium carrots, diced
1 tablespoon balsamic vinegar
1½ teaspoons vegetable bouillon powder
1½ teaspoons salt
1½ cups green peas, or 1 (10-ounce) package frozen peas, thawed
1 tablespoon potato starch dissolved in 1 tablespoon water

Mashed Root Vegetables
1½ pounds Yukon gold potatoes, peeled and diced medium
½ pound parsnip, peeled and diced medium
½ pound celery root, peeled and diced medium
½ pound rutabaga, peeled and diced medium
Pinch of salt
1 cup soy creamer
3 tablespoons nonhydrogenated margarine
½ teaspoon salt
¼ teaspoon white pepper

For the filling, heat the oil in a large stockpot or Dutch oven over medium heat, add the onion and garlic and sauté until the onion turns translucent, about 10 minutes. Add the Herbes de Provence, basil, curry powder and bay leaves and sauté until fragrant, 2 to 3 minutes. Add the split peas, lentils, tomato puree and vegetable broth; cover and simmer for 30 minutes. Add the diced carrots, vinegar, bouillon powder and salt and simmer uncovered, until the lentils, peas and carrots are tender, about 15 minutes. Turn off the heat. Add the peas and the dissolved potato starch, stir, and remove from the heat. Pour the mixture into a 9 by 13-inch baking dish and let cool. (At this point you may wrap the dish and refrigerate or freeze until needed.)

Preheat the oven to 350°F while you prepare the mashed root vegetables. Bring 8 cups of water to a boil in a large pot. Add the rutabaga and cook for 5 minutes. Add the potatoes, parsnip, and celery root and cook until the vegetables are tender, about 20 minutes. While the vegetables are cooking, heat the soy creamer and margarine in a small saucepan over medium-low heat (or in the microwave). Drain the vegetables, return them to the pot and mash them, adding the warm liquid as you mash. Add salt and white pepper to taste.

Spread the mashed root vegetables evenly over the lentil mixture. Bake until light golden brown on the top, 20 to 25 minutes, and serve.

Chef's Tip

The mashed root vegetables for the Shepherd's Pie topping also makes a wonderful side dish; adding color, flavor and nutrients to your meal. Try serving it whenever mashed potatoes would be served. You may choose your own vegetable combination; just use a total of 3 pounds, half potatoes and half other root vegetables.

Provençal Vegetable Quiche French

Chef Robin Robertson
Author, Presenter at Vegfest
Recipe from *Vegan Planet,* published by Harvard Common Press
www.robinrobertson.com

Silken tofu is used instead of eggs and cream in this light and luscious quiche. Mediterranean-spiced vegetables and a flaky crust make it a good choice for a light lunch or supper entrée served with a crisp green salad.

Serves 4 to 6

Crust
- 1 cup unbleached all-purpose flour
- ¼ cup chilled corn oil
- ¼ teaspoon salt
- 1 tablespoon cold water, or more as needed

Filling
- 1 tablespoon olive oil
- 1 leek, white part only, washed well and chopped
- 1½ cups chopped zucchini
- 1 cup chopped white mushrooms
- 1 cup finely chopped fresh or canned tomatoes, well drained
- 1 garlic clove, minced
- ¼ cup pitted black olives, chopped

- 1 teaspoon minced fresh marjoram leaves
- 1 teaspoon minced fresh basil leaves
- 1 teaspoon minced fresh tarragon leaves
- 1 teaspoon minced fresh parsley leaves
  Salt and freshly ground black pepper
- 2 cups drained and crumbled firm silken tofu
- 1 cup soymilk or other dairy-free milk
- 1 tablespoon Dijon mustard
- ⅛ teaspoon cayenne pepper
- ½ cup grated Parmesan-style nondairy cheese (optional)

To make the crust, combine the flour, corn oil and salt in a food processor and pulse until crumbly. With the machine running, add the water and process until the mixture forms a ball. Flatten the dough, wrap in plastic and refrigerate for at least 30 minutes. On a lightly floured work surface, roll out the dough to fit into a 10-inch quiche pan or pie plate. Line the pan or plate with the dough and trim the edges.

Preheat the oven to 375°F. To make the filling, heat the olive oil in a large skillet over medium heat. Add the leek, zucchini, mushrooms, tomatoes and garlic, and cook, stirring occasionally, until the vegetables soften and the liquid evaporates, about 7 minutes. Stir in the olives, herbs and salt and pepper to taste. Set aside.

In a food processor or blender, combine the tofu, soymilk, mustard, cayenne and salt to taste. Blend well. Spoon the vegetable mixture into the crust and sprinkle with the Parmesan-style cheese, if using. Pour the tofu mixture over all, distributing it evenly.

Bake until the filling is set and the top is golden brown, about 45 minutes. Let it rest for 5 minutes before cutting.

Reprinted with permission

Tofu Piroshki *Russian*

Chef Julia Terry
Author, Federal Way, WA
Recipe from *Conscious Vegetarian*, published by Julia Terry

This recipe makes a generous amount of piroshki, which is fortunate, because they're hard to stop eating. Piroshki freeze very well, wrapped airtight. Take them straight from the freezer as needed and warm them in a 300°F oven until soft.

Serves 8

Dough
1¾ cup warm water
1   tablespoon vegetable oil
1   tablespoon yeast
1½ cup unbleached all-purpose flour
1½ cup whole-wheat flour, plus some more
    for dusting the work surface
1   teaspoon salt
    Nonstick cooking spray
½   cup soymilk

Filling
1   tablespoon grapeseed oil
½   small head green cabbage, shredded
1   cup water
4   ounces baked tofu, crumbled
1   bunch scallions, chopped
½   bunch fresh cilantro, chopped
    Salt and ground black pepper

In a small bowl, stir together water, oil and yeast. Combine the all-purpose and whole-wheat flours and the salt in a large bowl, and add the yeast mixture slowly, mixing well with each addition. When all the water has been added, sprinkle some whole-wheat flour on your work surface, turn the dough out onto the flour and start kneading vigorously. Knead until the dough becomes elastic and swollen, about 10 minutes. The dough should be wet and sticky, so resist adding too much more flour; sprinkle the sides of the dough ball with just enough flour to be able to continue kneading. Spray a large, deep bowl with nonstick cooking spray, place the dough in the bowl and turn it over to coat both sides with spray. Cover with a towel and set in a warm (68 to 70°F), draft-free place, until it has doubled in size, 1 to 2 hours.

While the dough is rising, prepare the filling: Heat the oil in a large saucepan over low heat, add the cabbage, and sauté for 3 to 5 minutes. Add the water, increase the heat to medium, and continue to sauté, stirring often, until the cabbage is tender and the water has almost evaporated. Add the tofu, scallions, cilantro, and salt and pepper to taste, stir, cook just until heated through, and remove from the heat.

Spray 2 baking sheets with nonstick cooking spray. When the dough has doubled in size, punch it down and knead for 3 minutes (sprinkle a bit of flour on the sides of dough if needed). Roll the dough into a long rope, about 2 inches in diameter. Cut the rope into 1-inch pieces and roll each into a ball by pressing it firmly between the palms of your hands. As you make the dough balls, line them up on your work surface in the order you made them. Take the first ball you made (the dough should be relaxed and slightly puffy) and press it into a flat circle. Repeat with the other dough balls, again arranging them in the order in which you made them. Take the first circle you made and place a spoonful of filling on it, leaving a border around the edges for sealing. Lift both sides of the circle to enclose the filling, forming a half-circle. Pinch the seam at its midpoint. Pinch all along the edges of the piroshki, from the midpoint down to each end, to seal. Place the formed piroshki seam-side down on the prepared baking sheets. Leave 2 inches between each piroshki to allow space for expanding.

Cover the baking sheets with linen towels and leave for 1 hour to rest. Preheat the oven to 375°F. Uncover the piroshki and place them in the oven. Bake for 30 minutes or until light brown. Take out and brush the surface with the soymilk, using a pastry brush. Cover with the linen towel again, let rest for 20 minutes, and serve. If not eaten the same day, place the piroshki in a paper bag, then place in a plastic bag and cover with a towel. Piroshki will keep well at room temperature for 2 to 3 days.

Reprinted with permission

Calzones with Spinach, Pesto and Tofu Italian

Chef Heather Houck Resek, RD
Author, Presenter at Vegfest
Recipe from *Fix it Fast*, published by Review & Herald Publishing Association
www.vegetarianadvantage.com

These popular portable pockets are perfect to make ahead for picnics and lunches.

Serves 8

1 tablespoon olive oil, plus more for brushing on calzones	½ cup pesto
1 medium onion, chopped	½ teaspoon salt
2 cloves garlic, minced	1 recipe pizza dough or 2 pounds frozen whole wheat bread dough, thawed
1 (12-14 ounce) package firm tofu	
1 (10-ounce) package frozen chopped spinach, thawed and squeezed dry	4 cups spaghetti or marinara sauce, homemade or commercially prepared
1½ cups shredded mozzarella-style nondairy cheese	

Adjust the oven racks to the lower- and upper-middle positions. Heat the oven to 450°F. Line 2 large baking sheets with parchment paper or sprinkle with cornmeal to prevent sticking.

Heat the oil in a large skillet over medium heat, add the onion and garlic, and sauté until the onions are soft and translucent, about 10 minutes. Stir in the tofu, spinach, cheese, pesto and salt.

Divide the dough into 8 equal pieces, and cover with a damp cloth. Working with one piece at a time, stretch the dough into an 8-inch circle. Place about ½ cup of the filling on the lower half of the circle, leaving about a ½-inch border. Fold the top half of the dough over the filling to make a half-circle. Press the edges together with your fingers, then crimp them with a fork to seal them shut. Place 4 calzones on each prepared baking sheet. Brush the calzones with olive oil. Bake until crisp and golden brown, 20 to 25 minutes, rotating the baking sheets halfway through baking. While the calzones bake, heat the spaghetti sauce and serve the calzones warm with sauce on the side for dipping. The calzones may be stored up to 1 week in the refrigerator or wrapped well and frozen up to 3 months.

Eggplant Rollotini *Italian*

Ten Mercer
10 Mercer St, Seattle, WA (206) 691-3723

These delicious rolls are easily made if you take advantage of high-quality prepared foods, such as jarred roasted peppers, tapenade and marinara sauce. Be aware that tapenade often contains anchovies; check the label.

Serves 4

8 ounces firm tofu, crumbled

3 tablespoons fresh basil chopped

3 tablespoons olive tapenade, homemade *(see page 146)*, or commercially prepared

1 tablespoon chopped roasted red bell pepper

½ teaspoon kosher salt

½ teaspoon black pepper

2 cups flour

1 large eggplant, sliced lengthwise into ¼-inch-thick slices

4 tablespoons olive oil, plus more if necessary

2 cups marinara sauce (homemade or commercially prepared)

2 tablespoons basil chiffonade *(see page 138)*

1 cup grated Parmesan-style nondairy cheese

Heat the oven to 400°F. Mix the tofu, chopped basil, olive tapenade, roasted pepper, salt and black pepper in a small bowl and place in the refrigerator to chill. Place the flour in a shallow dish and dredge the eggplant slices in the flour. Line a large plate with paper towels. Heat the olive oil in a large skillet over medium-high heat until shimmering and add as many of the eggplant slices as will fit; don't crowd them. Fry the eggplant slices, turning once, until they are pliable and golden brown on both sides. Remove the eggplant from the pan and set on the paper-towel-lined plate, then cook the remaining slices, replenishing the oil as necessary. Working with one slice at a time, place a heaping spoonful of the tofu mixture at one end of each eggplant slice and roll up the slice to enclose the filling. Place the stuffed eggplant rolls seam-side down in a baking pan and bake until heated through, about 10 minutes.

While the eggplant rolls are in the oven, warm the marinara sauce in a medium saucepan over low heat. To serve, spoon some of the marinara onto each plate, place a few eggplant rolls on each plate, and top with more marinara, the Parmesan-style cheese and the basil chiffonade.

Baked Eggplant Ratatouille French

Chef Louise Hagler
Author, Presenter at Vegfest
Recipe from *The New Farm Vegetarian Cookbook,* published by the Book Publishing Company

This takes time to prepare, but is well worth it. It's good hot or cold. Rolled up in crepes or yuba (sheets of dried bean curd), it's a good dinner dish.

Serves 2

1 small eggplant, peeled and sliced ¼ inch thick	1 green bell pepper, chopped
Salt	2 cloves garlic, minced
	Ground black pepper
2 tablespoons flour	4 tomatoes, chopped
¼ cup olive oil	¼ cup minced fresh parsley
1 medium onion, chopped	2 small zucchini, chopped

Preheat the oven to 350°F. Place the eggplant slices in a colander, sprinkle them with 1 teaspoon salt, cover and weight down, and let stand for 30 minutes. Drain the eggplant, dry it on a towel and cut the slices into quarters. Flour the eggplant pieces.

In a large skillet, heat half the oil over medium heat, add the eggplant pieces and sauté until tender and light brown, about 15 minutes; remove from the pan. Add the remaining oil to the pan, then add the onion, pepper and garlic, and sauté until softened. Place the tomatoes on top of the cooked vegetables, cover the pan and cook 5 minutes. Take the cover off, raise the heat and cook 5 minutes more. Stir in the minced parsley.

Spread a third of the tomato mixture on the bottom of a 2-quart casserole dish. Cover with a layer of sliced zucchini and half the eggplant. Add another third of the mixture, then the remaining eggplant and zucchini. Finish with the remaining tomatoes. Bake for about 30 minutes.

Reprinted with permission

Latvian Sauerkraut *Latvieshu Skabie kaposti*

Chef Julia Terry
Author, Federal Way, WA
Recipe from *Conscious Vegetarian,* published by Julia Terry

This sauerkraut tastes great with roasted potatoes or as a side dish with a grilled veggie sandwich. It can be stored for up to a week in the refrigerator.

Serves 4

1	tablespoon grapeseed oil
3	medium onions, diced
1	small head green cabbage, shredded
1	(12-ounce) jar sauerkraut, drained
2	medium Granny Smith apples, cored and sliced
2	cups tomato juice
¼	cup water
1	teaspoon caraway seeds

Heat the oil in a large, deep skillet over low heat, add the onions, and sauté them gently until soft, about 15 minutes. Add the cabbage, sauerkraut, apples, tomato juice and water, increase the heat to medium-low, and cook until the cabbage is tender (this may take up to 1 hour). Add the caraway seeds and turn off the heat. Let the flavors develop for 15 to 20 minutes. Serve warm or cold.

Reprinted with permission

Hungarian Bell Pepper Lecho

Chef Julia Terry
Author, Federal Way, WA
Recipe from *Conscious Vegetarian*, published by Julia Terry

This makes great vegetable side dish over any grains or a snack with dark rye bread or crackers. It can be sealed in two 1-quart jars, following normal canning procedures, and preserved for several months.

Serves 4 to 5

1	tablespoon soybean oil	1	cup chopped fresh parsley
1	onion, diced	2	tablespoons ground horseradish
4	large bell peppers of various colors, cut in very thin matchsticks	1	tablespoon olive oil
		1	teaspoon red pepper flakes
3	cups crushed tomatoes	3	bay leaves
4	cloves garlic, chopped		Salt and ground black pepper

Heat the oil in a large saucepan over medium-low heat, add the onions, and sauté until soft. Add the bell peppers, cover, and cook until tender, lifting the cover occasionally to stir the vegetables. If the vegetables seem too dry and start sticking to the pan, add 1 to 2 tablespoons water. Add the crushed tomatoes and cook 5 to 10 minutes, then stir in the garlic and remove from the heat. Add chopped parsley, horseradish, olive oil, pepper flakes, bay leaves, and salt and pepper to taste, and mix well. Let stand until cool and the flavors have melded, then remove the bay leaves and serve.

Reprinted with permission

Spanakopita Greek

Patty Pan Grill

5402 20th Avenue NW, Seattle, WA (206) 782-1558
Vegfest Chef Devra Gartenstein
Recipe from *The Accidental Vegan*, published by The Crossing Press

In this variation of a traditional Greek favorite, lentils add heft to the tangy, hearty filling nestled between the crispy layers of phyllo dough.

Serves 12

1 (10-ounce) package frozen spinach, or 1 bunch fresh spinach, cleaned and trimmed	1 package tofu (14 –16 ounces), soft or firm, crumbled
½ cup olive oil	2 teaspoons sea salt
1 onion, chopped	1 teaspoon dried dill
3–6 cloves garlic, minced	½ teaspoon anise seed (optional)
2 cups cooked lentils	1 (16-ounce) package phyllo dough, thawed if frozen
1–2 tablespoons lemon juice	

Preheat the oven to 375°F. Steam the spinach until it's thawed or wilted. Heat 1 tablespoon of the oil in a medium skillet, add the onion and garlic, and sauté until softened, then add the spinach, lentils, lemon juice, tofu, salt, dill and anise seed, if using.

Unroll the phyllo dough and cover with a damp cloth to keep it from drying out. Pour the remaining oil into a shallow dish. Use a pastry brush to brush a little of the oil onto the bottom of a 9 by 13-inch baking pan. Lay a sheet of phyllo dough over it, brush it with oil, and repeat with 10 to 12 sheets. Don't agonize if some sheets stick together. The final product will look fine.

Spread the filling over the first 10 to 12 sheets, then layer the remaining phyllo sheets on top of the filling, brushing each one with oil. With a sharp knife, score the spanakopita into 12 pieces, cutting just to the filling. Cover with aluminum foil, and bake for 15 minutes, then uncover and bake for another 10 minutes. Serve warm or cold.

Reprinted with permission

Lentil Pottage *Majadra, Lebanese*

Abou Karim
221 SW Pine Street, Portland, OR (503) 223-5058

This simple, yet satisfying, stew may be eaten hot or cold.

Serves 4 to 6

- 1   cup green or brown lentils, picked over and rinsed
- 4   cups water
- ½   cup olive or vegetable oil
- 1   large onion, chopped
- ½   cup rice
- ⅛   teaspoon pepper
- ⅛   teaspoon cumin
-     Salt

Rinse the lentils, place them in a medium pan with the water, cover, and bring to a boil over high heat. Reduce the heat to medium and cook for 20 minutes.

While the lentils are cooking, heat the oil in a medium skillet over medium heat, add the onion and sauté until light golden brown, 10 to 15 minutes. Add the onions with their oil, the rice, pepper, cumin, and salt to taste to the lentils. Cover and cook for 20 minutes, stirring occasionally. Serve immediately or let cool. The mixture will thicken as it cools.

Fresh Herb Stew *Khoresh-e-Ghormeh Sabzi, Persian*

Chef Omid Roustaei, MA, ABS
Presenter at Vegfest and Monthly Dining Event chef
Faculty, School of Natural Cookery in Boulder, Colorado
PCC Cooks Culinary Instructor
www.members.aol.com/wholefoodschef/

The earthy flavors of black-eyed peas and mushrooms blend well with fresh herbs in this easy stew. Serve over Steamed Saffron Rice (page 168).

Serves 4 to 5

4 ounces baby spinach leaves	1 cup sliced white button mushrooms
1 small leek, white and light green parts only, chopped	2 teaspoons salt
	½ teaspoon pepper
1 cup fresh cilantro leaves	½ teaspoon turmeric
1 cup fresh parsley leaves	½ teaspoon cinnamon
½ cup olive oil	2 cups water
1 large onion, halved and sliced thin	1 (14½-ounce) can black-eyed peas
2 carrots, diced	Juice of 1 lime

Place the spinach, leek, cilantro and parsley in a food processor, process until finely chopped, and set aside.

Heat the oil in a medium saucepan over medium heat, add the onion, and sauté for 5 minutes. Add the carrots, mushrooms, salt, pepper, turmeric, cinnamon, and sauté for an additional 2 minutes. Add the chopped greens to the pot and cook, stirring constantly, for 5 minutes. Add the water, black-eyed peas and lime juice, stir well, and simmer over low heat for about 30 minutes. Serve.

Yellow Split Pea Stew with Tofu and Roasted Potatoes *Khoresh-e-Gheymeh, Persian*

Chef Omid Roustaei, MA, ABS

Presenter at Vegfest and Monthly Dining Event chef
Faculty, School of Natural Cookery in Boulder, Colorado
PCC Cooks Culinary Instructor
www.members.aol.com/wholefoodschef/

This stew has a wonderful depth of flavor and will fill your house with a heavenly aroma as it cooks. Don't be put off by the long list of ingredients; many of them are spices, which merely need to be measured into a bowl. Serve over Steamed Saffron Rice (page 168).

Serves 6

Potatoes and Tofu
- 4 teaspoons salt
- 1 tablespoon turmeric
- 1 teaspoon ground cumin
- ½ teaspoon ground ginger
- ½ teaspoon ground cinnamon
- ½ teaspoon ground coriander
- ½ cup olive oil
- 1 pound potatoes, diced
- 1 package (14–16 ounces) firm tofu, diced

Yellow Split Peas
- 1 cup yellow split peas, picked over and rinsed
- 2 teaspoons turmeric
- ½ teaspoon ground saffron
- ½ teaspoon ground cumin
- ¼ teaspoon ground ginger
- ¼ teaspoon ground cinnamon
- ¼ teaspoon ground coriander
- 4 tablespoons olive oil
- 2 onions, sliced
- 2 pounds whole peeled tomatoes
- 1 tablespoon tomato paste
  Juice of 1 lemon
- 2 teaspoons salt (or more to taste)
- ½ teaspoon ground black pepper

For the potatoes and tofu, adjust the oven racks to the upper- and lower-middle positions and preheat the oven to 375°F. Have ready 2 rimmed baking sheets.

Measure the salt, turmeric, cumin, ginger, cinnamon and coriander into a small bowl and stir to combine. Pour ¼ cup of the oil into a medium bowl, add half of the spice mix, and stir to blend. Add the diced potatoes, toss well, and transfer to the first rimmed baking sheet. Pour the remaining ¼ cup oil into the empty bowl, add the remaining spice mix, and stir to blend. Add the diced tofu, toss well, and transfer to the second rimmed baking sheet. Place both baking sheets in the oven and cook until the potatoes are tender, about 30 minutes.

While the potatoes and tofu are baking, place the peas in a large saucepan with 8 cups water and boil, uncovered, over medium high heat until done, 10 to 15 minutes (don't overcook). Drain in a colander, saving the liquid.

Measure the turmeric, saffron, cumin, ginger, cinnamon and coriander into a small bowl. Heat the oil in a large stockpot or Dutch oven over medium heat, add the onions and sauté for about 5 minutes. Add the spice mixture and sauté for an additional 2 minutes. Add the tomatoes, tomato paste, cooked split peas, 3 cups of cooking liquid from the split peas, lemon juice, salt and pepper. Simmer for about 15 minutes.

Add the tofu and potatoes to the yellow pea mixture and simmer for about 10 minutes. Serve over steamed basmati rice.

Seitan Stew with Walnuts and Pomegranate
Khoresh-e-Fesenjoon, Persian

Chef Omid Roustaei, MA, ABS
Presenter at Vegfest and Monthly Dining Event chef
Faculty, School of Natural Cookery in Boulder, Colorado
PCC Cooks Culinary Instructor
www.members.aol.com/wholefoodschef/

During the slow cooking process, the walnuts release their natural oils, which creates a lustrous creamy sauce. Pomegranate paste is sold in Indian and Middle Eastern markets. Serve over Steamed Saffron Rice (page 168).

Serves 6

2 cups walnut pieces	1 tablespoon lemon juice
½ cup pomegranate paste	½ cup sugar, or more to taste
3 cups hot water	2 teaspoons salt
4 tablespoons olive oil	¼ teaspoon ground saffron
1 large onion, diced	
1 (16-ounce) package chicken-style seitan, shredded *(see below)*	

In a food processor, pulse the walnuts until finely ground. (Don't overdo it, or you will have walnut butter). Set aside.

In a small bowl combine the pomegranate paste and water, stirring until the paste is dissolved. Heat the oil in a large saucepan over medium heat, add the onions and seitan, and sauté for about 5 minutes. Add the ground walnuts and stir well. Add the pomegranate water, lemon juice, sugar, salt and saffron. Bring to a boil, cover, reduce the heat to low, and simmer for 1 hour, stirring occasionally. Serve.

―――

Seitan
Seitan (pronounced SAY-tan), also known as "wheat-meat," is made from wheat gluten and is quite high in protein and low in fat. Seitan has a chewy texture and mild taste that allows it to absorb a variety of flavors, making it an ideal substitute for meat in stews, spaghetti sauces, etc. You can make your own seitan or purchase prepared seitan at natural food stores, where it is sold refrigerated in plastic-wrapped packages or in tubs.

Seitan à la Grecque Greek

Chef Tanya Petrovna
Author, Presenter at Vegfest
www.nativefoods.com

This easy seitan dish, presented at Vegfest, is zesty with the bright flavors of lemon, parsley, and tomato. Serve it with steamed greens and the grain of your choice.

Serves 4

Quick Tofu Feta
- 4 ounces firm tofu, chopped in ½ inch cubes
- ¼ cup olive oil
- ¼ cup lemon juice
- 1 teaspoon sea salt
- ¼ teaspoon dried oregano

Seitan
- ¼ cup olive oil
- 12 ounces seitan, sliced thin
- 1 medium tomato, chopped
- 2 cloves garlic, chopped
- 8–10 kalamata olives, pitted and sliced
- 6 artichoke hearts, sliced
- 1 teaspoon sea salt
- ¼ teaspoon black pepper
- ¼ cup chopped fresh parsley, plus more for garnish
  Lemon slices for garnish

To make the quick tofu feta, whisk together the olive oil, lemon juice, salt, and oregano in a small bowl, add the tofu cubes, toss to coat the tofu with the liquid, and marinate for 20 minutes. For the seitan, heat the olive oil in a medium skillet over medium heat, add the seitan and sauté until lightly browned. Add the tomato and garlic and simmer for 1 minute. Add the olives, artichoke hearts, tofu feta, salt, pepper and parsley and mix lightly. Garnish with lemon slices and a sprinkling of parsley, and serve.

Steamed Saffron Rice Persian

Chef Omid Roustaei, MA, ABS

Presenter at Vegfest and Monthly Dining Event chef
Faculty, School of Natural Cookery in Boulder, Colorado
PCC Cooks Culinary Instructor
www.members.aol.com/wholefoodschef/

The lovely aroma and delicate flavor of this rice dish pairs perfectly with any of the Persian stews: Yellow Split Pea Stew with Tofu and Roasted Potatoes, Fresh Herb Stew, or Seitan Stew with Walnuts and Pomegranate.

Serves 8

4	cups white basmati rice
2	teaspoons salt
¼	cup olive oil
	Pinch of saffron dissolved in 2 tablespoons hot water

Wash the rice thoroughly and place it in a large saucepan. Add 8 cups water, the salt, and oil, and bring to a boil over high heat. Cook uncovered, until the rice is slightly soft, 10 to 15 minutes. Most of the water should be gone by now. Off the heat, pull the rice away from the edges of the pot and heap it in the center, forming it into a cone shape. Cover the pot, return it to medium-low heat and cook until done, 30 to 40 minutes. Pour the saffron/water mixture over the top of the rice. Take it off the heat and allow to cool for about 5 minutes without lifting the lid.

Falafel *Middle Eastern*

Patty Pan Grill

5402 20th Avenue NW, Seattle, WA (206) 782-1558
Vegfest Chef Devra Gartenstein
Recipe from *The Accidental Vegan*, published by The Crossing Press

Falafel is one of my favorite sandwiches. The chickpea balls are traditionally deep fried, but I prefer to bake them, so they're lower in fat, and so the whole operation is much less messy.

Serves 4

2	cups cooked chickpeas	1	teaspoon sea salt
½	cup tahini	½	cup water
¼	cup chopped fresh parsley	4	loaves pita bread
	Juice of 1 lemon (about 3 tablespoons)	4	leaves crisp lettuce, torn in strips
2	tablespoons olive oil	2	tomatoes, chopped
2	cloves garlic, minced		

Preheat the oven to 375°F. Lightly coat a rimmed baking sheet with nonstick cooking spray. Place the chickpeas, ¼ cup of the tahini, 2 tablespoons of the parsley, half of the lemon juice, 1 tablespoon of the olive oil, the garlic and ½ teaspoon of the salt in a food processor. Process to a coarse paste, scraping down the sides of the workbowl as necessary. Form this mixture into 1-inch balls (you should have at least 16), place on the baking sheet and bake for 20 minutes.

Meanwhile, for the sauce, whisk together the remaining tahini, parsley, lemon juice, olive oil and sea salt in a small bowl, along with the water.

Cut a strip off each loaf of pita bread, then open the pocket and stuff it with 4 balls, some of the lettuce and tomato, and drizzle some of the sauce on top.

Reprinted with permission

Eggplant Salad *Patlican, Middle Eastern*

Mezé
935 6th Street South, Kirkland, WA (425) 828-3923

The flavors in this chunky salad are similar to Baba Ghanoush, the classic roasted eggplant spread. It can be served as a sandwich filling, stuffed into pita pockets, or over couscous.

Serves 4

4	small eggplants
2	large tomatoes, diced
½–¾	green bell pepper, diced
⅓	red onion, diced
½	cup lemon juice
⅔	cup olive oil
	Salt and ground black pepper
2	tablespoons chopped fresh parsley

Grill or roast the eggplants: To grill the eggplants, light the grill and adjust the flame to medium-low. Pierce the eggplants in a few places with a fork. Place the eggplants on the grill and cook, turning often, until the skin is charred and the flesh is soft, 20 to 30 minutes. To roast the eggplants, heat the oven to 400°F. Pierce the eggplants in a few places with a fork, place them on a rimmed baking sheet and bake, turning once, until the skin is dark and the flesh is soft, 30 to 40 minutes. Allow them to cool slightly.

Peel the grilled eggplants, dice them in large cubes, and place the eggplant cubes in a large bowl. Add the tomatoes, green pepper and onion. In a small bowl, whisk together the lemon juice and olive oil with salt and pepper to taste. Pour the dressing over the vegetables, and mix all the ingredients together carefully, so the vegetables do not become mushy. Sprinkle with the parsley.

Red Lentil Stew *Missira, Ethiopian*

Horn of Africa

3939 NE Martin Luther King Boulevard, Portland, OR (503) 331-9844

Garam masala is a blend of spices that usually includes cinnamon, black pepper, cumin and coriander, among others. Serve this thick stew with any kind of bread or rice.

Serves 4

2	tablespoons canola oil
1	medium onion, chopped
6	medium cloves garlic, chopped
3	tablespoons paprika
1	cup red lentils
2	cups water
1–2	teaspoons garam masala

Heat the oil in a large saucepan over medium heat, add the onion and garlic, and sauté until they turn golden brown. Add the paprika, lentils and water, cover and simmer for 10 minutes. Add the garam masala, cover and simmer for another 20 to 25 minutes.

Moroccan Chickpea Stew

D'Anna's Deli Café
1307 11th Street, Bellingham, WA (360) 752-3390

Marinara sauce, lemon juice and raisins add bright notes to this savory stew. Serve over couscous or brown rice; if you'd like to serve this family-style, spoon the couscous or rice onto a large platter, make a depression in the center, and ladle the stew into the "well."

Serves 4 to 6

3	tablespoons extra-virgin olive oil	¼	teaspoon ground cloves
2	medium onions, chopped	¼	teaspoon red chili flakes
3–4	garlic cloves, minced	4	cups marinara sauce
1	red bell pepper, chopped	¼	cup nonalcoholic red wine (optional)
1	medium eggplant, chopped	1	cup canned chickpeas
1	medium zucchini, chopped	½	cup raisins
1	teaspoon cinnamon	2	tablespoons lemon juice
1	teaspoon paprika		Salt and ground pepper to taste
1	teaspoon ground cumin	¼	cup chopped parsley

Heat the oil in a large stockpot or Dutch oven over medium heat, add the onions, garlic, pepper, eggplant and zucchini, and sauté for about 5 minutes. Add the cinnamon, paprika, cumin, cloves and chili flakes and for sauté 2 minutes longer. Add the marinara sauce and wine, if using. Simmer, uncovered, until the sauce is thick and the vegetables are tender, about 20 minutes. Add the chickpeas, raisins and salt and pepper and lemon juice and stir to incorporate and heat through. Ladle into individual bowls or a large platter, sprinkle the chopped parsley over the top, and serve.

Nigerian Groundnut Stew with Tempeh

Chef Robin Robertson
Author, Presenter at Vegfest
Recipe from *366 Healthful Ways to Cook Tofu,* published by Penguin
www.robinrobertson.com

*In Africa, as well as other places, the peanut is known as the groundnut and is a popular
ingredient in many appetizing dishes, like this high-protein casserole.*

Serves 4

2   tablespoons corn oil
1   pound tempeh, poached *(see box)*
    and cut into 1-inch dice
1   large onion, chopped
2   green bell peppers, chopped
1   clove garlic, minced

1   cup peanut butter, or more as needed
1   cup vegetable broth, or more as needed
1   large tomato, peeled and chopped
½   teaspoon salt
⅛   teaspoon freshly ground black pepper
1   cup white or brown rice

Preheat the oven to 350°F. Heat the oil in a large skillet over medium-high heat. Add the
tempeh and sauté until browned on all sides, about 5 minutes. Remove with a slotted spoon
and place in a casserole dish. In the same skillet, cook the onion, bell peppers and garlic until
the onion is transparent, about 5 minutes. Add this to the casserole.

Place the peanut butter in a saucepan and add the broth slowly, stirring to make a thick
creamy sauce. Place the saucepan over medium heat, add the tomato, salt and pepper,
and simmer gently for 2 minutes; pour over the tempeh and vegetables in the casserole. If
the sauce is too thin, add more peanut butter; if it's too thick, add more stock. Cover and
bake for 30 minutes. While the casserole is in the oven, cook the rice according to package
directions. Spoon the tempeh casserole over the rice and serve.

Chef's Tip
*Poaching commercially prepared tempeh before using it in a recipe improves its flavor and
digestibility. Slice or cube tempeh according to individual recipe, or leave in slabs, depending
on use. Place the tempeh in a saucepan, add enough water to cover it and bring to a boil.
Reduce the heat to medium and simmer for 10 minutes. Remove the tempeh from the water
and proceed with the recipe.*

Reprinted with permission

Moroccan-Spiced Fava Bean Stew

Chef Robin Robertson
Author, Presenter at Vegfest
Recipe from *Vegan Planet,* published by Harvard Common Press
www.robinrobertson.com

Fragrant spices and dried fruits lend a Moroccan flavor to this hearty stew made with meaty fava beans. Fresh favas can be difficult to find and are time-consuming to prepare, since they need to be blanched and peeled before cooking. Dried, frozen or canned fava beans may be found in specialty markets and some supermarkets. If favas are unavailable, substitute lima beans

Serves 4

½	cup mixed dried fruit	8	ounces green beans, ends trimmed, cut into 1 inch pieces
¼	cup raisins or dried currants	2	cups vegetable broth
1	tablespoon olive oil	1½	cups cooked fava beans, or 1 (15-ounce) can, drained and rinsed
1	large sweet yellow onion, chopped		
1	large carrot, diced	½	cup frozen green peas, thawed
1	large garlic clove, minced		Salt and freshly ground black pepper
1	teaspoon ground cumin	1	tablespoon minced fresh cilantro or parsley leaves
1	teaspoon ground cinnamon		
1	(14½-ounce) can diced tomatoes, drained and chopped		

Bring 2 cups of water to a boil in a small saucepan or in the microwave. Place the dried fruit and raisins in a small heatproof bowl. Add boiling water to cover and soak for 20 minutes to soften. Drain and set aside.

Heat the olive oil in a large saucepan over medium heat. Add the onion and carrot, cover and cook until softened, about 5 minutes. Add the garlic, cumin and cinnamon and cook, stirring, for 30 seconds. Add the tomatoes, green beans and stock and bring to the boil. Reduce the heat to low and simmer until the vegetables are tender, about 15 minutes.

Add the favas, peas, fruit and salt and pepper to taste. Simmer, uncovered, until the flavors are blended and the desired consistency is achieved, about 10 minutes. Sprinkle with the cilantro and serve over couscous or rice.

Ethiopian-Style Collard Greens *Raafu*

Horn of Africa
3939 NE Martin Luther King Boulevard, Portland, OR (503) 331-9844

Collards may look tough, but they have a mild flavor similar to cabbage, and they cook fairly quickly. Serve this simple side dish with pita, French, or any other kind of bread. An Ethiopian bread, such as Biddeena or injera, would be ideal.

Serves 4

- 1 tablespoon canola oil
- 1 medium onion, chopped
- 2 medium cloves garlic, chopped
- 1 bunch fresh collard greens, tough stems removed, leaves chopped.
   Salt to taste

Heat the oil in a large stockpot or Dutch oven over medium heat. Add the onion and sauté until golden, about 10 minutes. Add the garlic and sauté, stirring frequently, for 5 minutes longer. Reduce heat to low, add the collard greens and enough water to cover the bottom of the pot, 1 to 2 cups. Cover and steam for 10 to 15 minutes. Add salt to taste and serve.

Vegetable Korma

Mayuri Indian Cuisine

15400 NE 20th Street, Bellevue, WA (425) 641-4442
www.mayuriseattle.com

A freshly ground spice blend makes this dish special, and is easy to do. Serve this dish over basmati rice or accompany with whole-wheat Indian flatbread, such as roti.

Serves 4 to 6

Vegetables
1	(16-ounce) package mixed frozen vegetables, or 1 pound fresh mixed vegetables, such as cauliflower, carrots, peas, beans, cut into bite-size pieces
1	tablespoon oil
2	large onions, chopped
2	tomatoes, chopped
2	teaspoons salt
1	teaspoon chili powder
2	cups water

Masala paste
¼	cup grated coconut
2	tablespoons chopped cashew nuts
2	tablespoons fennel seeds
4	cloves garlic
4	dry red chiles
2	cardamom pods, broken open, outer layer discarded, black seeds reserved
2	cloves
1	tablespoon chopped fresh ginger
1	cup water
	Juice of 1 lemon
2	tablespoons chopped fresh cilantro

In a large saucepan, bring 8 cups of water to a boil, add the mixed vegetables and boil for 2 to 3 minutes; drain and set aside. Heat the oil in a large saucepan over medium heat, add the onion and sauté for 5 minutes, then add the tomato and sauté for an additional 5 to 10 minutes. Add the cooked vegetables, salt, chili powder and water, bring to a simmer and cook for 10 minutes.

Meanwhile, place the coconut, nuts, fennel, garlic, chiles, cardamom seeds, cloves, ginger, and water in a blender. Puree to form a paste. Add the masala paste to the vegetables in the saucepan and cook for 5 more minutes, adding more water if necessary to achieve a sauce-like consistency. Remove from heat, sprinkle with lemon juice and cilantro, and serve.

Chickpea Curry *Channa Masala*

Mayuri Indian Cuisine
15400 NE 20th Street, Bellevue, WA (425) 641-4442
www.mayuriseattle.com

Serve this savory and hearty bean dish over rice, such as Saffron Rice (page 190), or with flatbread.

Serves 5 to 6

2 tablespoons vegetable oil	1 teaspoon chili powder
5 cloves	Salt
2 cinnamon sticks	3 medium yellow onions, chopped
3 cardamom pods	2 medium or 3 small waxy potatoes, diced small
1 (4-ounce) piece ginger, sliced	5 medium tomatoes, diced
3 medium cloves garlic, minced or pressed through a garlic press	3 green chiles, diced
2 teaspoons ground coriander	1 (14½-ounce) can chickpeas
2 teaspoons ground cumin	Juice of 1 lemon
2 teaspoons paprika	2 tablespoons chopped fresh cilantro
1 teaspoon turmeric powder	

Heat the oil in a large, heavy skillet over medium heat. Add the cloves, cinnamon, and cardamom, and sauté until fragrant, 1 minute. Add the ginger and garlic and sauté for 1 more minute. Add the coriander, cumin, paprika, turmeric, chili powder and salt to taste, and stir to blend. Add the onions and sauté until light golden brown, about 8 minutes. Add the potatoes and sauté, stirring occasionally, for about 8 minutes, then add the tomatoes and chiles. Cover and cook for 10 minutes. Add the chickpeas, stir, and cook for 5 minutes. Sprinkle with the lemon juice and cilantro and serve.

Indian Kale and Tofu

Holy Cow Café
EMU Building C, University of Oregon, Eugene, OR (541) 346-2562
www.holycowcafe.com

This is a robust vegan version of Saag Paneer, the ubiquitous creamed spinach dish. It's delicious served with hot naan bread.

Serves 2 to 3

1½ cups water	3 cloves garlic, minced
1 pound kale, stems separated from leaves, stems diced, leaves chopped	1¼ teaspoons ginger powder
	¾ teaspoon ground cumin
1½ tablespoons vegetable oil	¾ teaspoon ground coriander
½ medium onion, chopped	½ teaspoon cayenne
10 ounces firm tofu, cut into small cubes	Pinch nutmeg
	Pinch ground cloves
1⅓ cups water	2 medium tomatoes, diced
3 teaspoons lemon juice	¼ cup water
1¼ teaspoon salt	1½ ounces potato flakes

Bring the water to a boil in a medium stockpot or Dutch oven. Add the kale stems, cover, and cook until almost tender, then add the leaves and cook, stirring occasionally, until tender. Place the kale in a food processor and process until almost smooth. Reserve.

In a medium skillet, heat the oil over medium heat. Add the onion and sauté until golden. Add the tofu, water, 2 teaspoons of the lemon juice and ¾ teaspoon of the salt. Bring to a boil, then simmer over low heat for 10 minutes. Add the garlic, ginger, cumin, coriander, cayenne, nutmeg, cloves and the remaining ½ teaspoon salt. Continue cooking until the pan begins to dry out. Add the tomatoes, a scant ¼ cup of water, the remaining teaspoon of lemon juice, the potato flakes and the pureed kale. Cook for 15 minutes more. Serve.

Potato and Cauliflower Curry Aloo Gobhi

Namasthe Cuisine of India
16650 Redmond Way, Redmond, WA (425) 558-7858

Use any small round boiling potato for this delicious classic Indian recipe.

Serves 6

1 small onion, chopped	1½ teaspoons salt
3 cloves garlic, chopped	1½ teaspoons turmeric
3 tablespoons canola oil	¾ teaspoon chili powder
Cumin seeds to taste	1 tablespoon ground ginger
2 medium tomatoes, sliced	1½ teaspoons garam masala *(see below)*
2 pounds cauliflower, cut into small florets	¼ cup fresh cilantro leaves, chopped
1 pound potatoes, peeled and diced small	2 scallions, white and light green parts, chopped

Heat the oil in a large, heavy skillet over medium-high heat. Add the onion and garlic and sauté until the onion is translucent, about 5 minutes. Add cumin seeds to taste and sauté for 7 minutes. Add the tomatoes and cook for an additional 3 to 4 minutes. Add the cauliflower, potatoes, salt, turmeric, red chili powder and ginger. Cover and cook for 15 to 20 minutes, stirring occasionally. When cooked, add the garam masala and stir to combine thoroughly. Top with the cilantro and scallions and serve.

Garam Masala
Garam masala is a blend of spices, used throughout South Asia, whose ingredients may vary, but usually include cinnamon, black pepper, cumin and coriander, among others. It is generally added in a small quantity at the end of cooking to add a subtle flavor to the dish.

Cabbage Curry

Chef Sid Andersen
Presenter at Vegfest
Masala Maza Foods
www.masalamaza.com

This is an easy, quick dry curry that can be made with any vegetable like carrots, broccoli, cauliflower, etc. in place of the cabbage.

Serves 4

1	tablespoon canola oil
1	teaspoon brown mustard seeds
1	teaspoon cumin seeds
2	teaspoons curry powder
2	teaspoons chopped fresh ginger
½	medium cabbage, chopped
½	teaspoon sea salt
¼	cup chopped fresh cilantro

Heat the oil over medium-high heat in a wok-style pan until shimmering. Add the mustard and cumin seeds, and cook until they pop. Immediately add the curry powder and ginger, and then stir in the cabbage and salt. Cook, stirring continuously, for 2 minutes. Remove from the heat, add the fresh cilantro, and serve.

Pumpkin Curry

Silence Heart Nest
3510 Fremont Place N, Seattle, WA (206) 524-4008

A rich and fragrant winter dish. Try it over Indian Saffron Rice (page 190).

Serves 6

1 cup dried unsweetened coconut, soaked in ¾ cup warm water
12 cloves garlic, chopped (about ¼ cup)
½–1 tablespoon Dijon mustard
½ teaspoon peppercorns
½ teaspoon turmeric
1½ teaspoons salt

2 medium onions, sliced
½ jalapeño pepper (include seeds to taste)
½ cinnamon stick
5 pounds pumpkin or butternut squash, peeled, seeded, and cut into 1-inch cubes
1 (14-ounce) can coconut milk

Place the coconut, garlic, mustard, peppercorns, turmeric and salt in a food processor or blender and blend briefly. Add the onions and jalapeño, and blend for a few seconds more.

Pour the mixture into a large deep skillet or Dutch oven, add the cinnamon stick and cook over medium heat, stirring frequently, for 5 minutes. If needed, add water to prevent sticking. Add the pumpkin to the sauce. Cover and cook until tender, about 20 minutes, removing lid to stir periodically. When the pumpkin is tender, stir in the coconut milk, reduce the heat to low, and cook, stirring, until the coconut milk is heated and the flavors are blended, about 5 minutes. Adjust the seasonings to taste and serve.

Spicy Yellow Dal *Rasam*

The LocoMotive

291 E 5th Street, Eugene, OR (541) 465-4754
www.thelocomotive.com

Several cuts above your average dal, this recipe can be used over rice as a main course. Try it with Pulao Rice (page 189).

Serves 6

1 cup toor dal *(see facing page)*	1 teaspoon ground cumin
5 cups water	1 teaspoon ground coriander
½ teaspoon ground turmeric	¾ teaspoon black pepper
2 tablespoons corn oil	¼ cup finely chopped fresh cilantro
1 teaspoon whole black mustard seeds	2 tablespoons juice from 1 lemon
1 medium jalapeño pepper (or to taste), chopped fine	2 teaspoons salt, or to taste
2 large ripe tomatoes, diced, or 1 cup canned diced tomatoes	

Spread the dal on a large plate and inspect it, discarding any small stones or other foreign objects. Place the dal in a strainer and rinse under cold water until the water runs clear. (If using oily toor dal, rinse in hot water.)

In a large, heavy pot, combine the dal, 2 cups of water, turmeric and 1 tablespoon of the oil. Bring the mixture to a boil over medium heat. Reduce heat to a lively simmer and cook covered until very soft, about one hour, stirring occasionally and adding a little water if necessary. Watch carefully at the end of cooking time for sticking. Mash to a paste in the pot using a potato masher or heavy spoon. Remove from the heat and set aside.

Heat the remaining tablespoon of oil in a large, heavy saucepan over medium heat. Add the mustard seeds and jalapeño and fry together, stirring for 1 minute. Add the remaining 3 cups of water to this mixture and bring to a boil. Add the tomatoes, cumin, coriander and black pepper and stir well. Return to a boil, reduce the heat and simmer for 5 minutes.

Add the spiced mixture to the mashed dal, stir and bring back to a boil. Remove from heat and add the chopped cilantro. Gradually stir in the lemon juice and salt, tasting as you go, until you like the flavor balance. (Salt and acidity are easily confused; add each carefully to avoid too much of either.)

Toor dal

Toor dal is a type of yellow lentil, usually available at Asian or Indian grocery stores. Yellow split peas make a tasty substitute, although they won't taste quite the same.

Spicy Indian Stuffing *Bread Khichadi*

Plainfields' Mayur
852 SW 21st Street, Portland, OR (503) 223-2995
www.plainfields.com

Here is an interesting Indian dish. Serve with soy yogurt and lemon wedges.

Serves 6

⅓	cup vegetable oil	½	cup green peas
½	teaspoon mustard seeds	1	teaspoon salt
1	teaspoon turmeric	1	tablespoon sugar
2	green chiles, sliced thin	8	cups cubed bread (about 10 large slices)
½	cup peanuts		Unsweetened flaked coconut
1	large onion, diced		Fresh cilantro leaves
1	medium tomato, diced		

Heat the oil in a large saucepan over medium-high heat. When the oil is hot, add the mustard seeds, turmeric and chiles. Add the peanuts and cook until slightly brown. Add the onion and cook until soft, about 10 minutes. Add the tomato, peas, salt, sugar and bread. Toss until all the bread is coated. Cover and steam 3 minutes. Toss again, cover and cook for 3 more minutes. You can either serve this soft, or cook until more crisp. Garnish with coconut and cilantro.

Spicy Cream of Wheat *Upmaa*

Plainfields' Mayur
852 SW 21st Street, Portland, OR (503) 223-2995
www.plainfields.com

This dish is traditionally served for breakfast or with afternoon tea, but its savory flavors make it well suited as a dinner side dish. It is very nutritious, low in fat and quick to make.

Serves 4

- 1 cup Cream of Wheat
- 1 tablespoon oil
- 1 teaspoon cumin seeds
- 2 dried red chiles (optional)
- ½ cup peanuts
- 1 teaspoon salt
- 1 medium onion, diced fine
- 2–3 cups boiling water
  - Chopped fresh cilantro leaves
  - Plain soy yogurt

Toast the Cream of Wheat in a medium saucepan pan until it turns slightly yellow-brown. Remove from the pan and set aside. Heat the oil in the pan, add the cumin and chiles, if desired, and sauté 5 to 10 seconds. Add the peanuts, salt and onions and cook until the onions are golden brown.

Add the toasted Cream of Wheat and 2 cups of the boiling water. The cereal will absorb the water. Stir, reduce the heat to medium-low, cover and cook for 5 minutes, until the cereal feels soft to the touch and tastes "done." Add up to 1 more cup of water, if needed to get the cereal to the right consistency. Garnish with the cilantro and serve with plain soy yogurt.

Lentil and Rice Pancakes with Spicy Potato Filling

Masala Dosa

Plainfields' Mayur

852 SW 21st Street, Portland, OR (503) 223-2995
www.plainfields.com

This classic South Indian food is nutritious, inexpensive, and easy to make; it's often eaten as breakfast or a snack, although it makes a good main course. Although the rice and dal require some advance preparation (they must soak for several hours) the batter stores well in the refrigerator for up to a week, so you can make dosa in a matter of minutes.

Serves 6

Batter

- 1   cup split white urid dal
    (see facing page)
- 2   cups rice
- 1   tablespoon salt
- 4   tablespoons vegetable oil,
    plus more for cooking the dosas

Filling

- 1   teaspoon mustard seeds
- 1   teaspoon turmeric
- 2   green chiles, sliced
- 1   medium onion, diced
- 1   pound boiling potatoes, cooked,
    peeled and cubed
- ½   cup fresh cilantro leaves, chopped

To make the batter, rinse the rice and dal in separate bowls. Cover with cold water and let them soak at room temperature for 8 to 10 hours, then drain them. Blend the rice into a paste with 6 tablespoons water. Place it in a deep bowl. Blend the dal with 6 tablespoons water until creamy. Combine the rice and dal batters and 2 teaspoons of the salt, cover and let it sit for 10 to 12 hours in a warm place to ferment.

For the filling, heat the oil in a large skillet over medium-high heat until shimmering. Add the mustard seeds. Be careful; they will pop. Immediately add the turmeric and chiles. Next, add the onion and remaining teaspoon of salt, and cook until the onion is translucent. Add the potatoes and cook for five minutes. Remove from heat and stir in the cilantro leaves. To make the pancakes (dosa), heat a heavy skillet (preferably nonstick) over medium heat until hot. Pour ½ cup of the batter into the center of the skillet, and with the back of a ladle, starting from the center, spread out the batter very thin, using a circular motion. Dribble a little oil around the edges and cook until crisp. Spoon some of the filling in the center and roll up. Repeat with the remaining batter and filling.

Urid Dal

Urid dal is made from black lentils that have been split and skinned, so that only the white interior remains. It is sold at Indian markets.

Indian Hash Browns *Potato Khis*

Plainfields' Mayur
852 SW 21st Street, Portland, OR (503) 223-2995
www.plainfields.com

After you make this dish, hash browns will never be the same. It is traditionally fried crisp, garnished with chopped cilantro and accompanied by fresh soy yogurt and lemon wedges.

Serves 4

4	large waxy potatoes (par-boiled, half-cooked, then peeled and grated)	
½	cup finely ground peanuts	
1	tablespoon sugar	
2	teaspoons salt	
⅓	cup oil	

1	teaspoon cumin seeds
1–2	green chiles, sliced fine
4	tablespoons chopped fresh cilantro
4	tablespoons grated coconut
	Soy yogurt
	Lemon wedges

Bring 8 cups water to a boil in a large saucepan, add the potatoes, and cook until half-done, about 15 minutes. Cool, peel, and grate on the large holes of a box grater. Place the grated potatoes in a bowl, add the peanuts, sugar and salt, and stir. In a large skillet, heat the oil over medium-high heat until hot, add the cumin seeds and fry for 5 seconds. Add the chiles and fry for 10 seconds. Add the potato mixture and stir. Cover, reduce heat to medium, and cook for 5 minutes. Uncover, stir and continue frying until crisp. Sprinkle chopped coriander and grated coconut over the top and serve, passing soy yogurt and fresh lemon wedges at the table.

Pulao Rice

Pabla Indian Cuisine
364 Renton Center Way SW, Renton, WA (425) 228-4625
www.pablacuisine.com

Here's a classic, and simple, Indian rice dish to accompany any of the stews in this chapter, such as Spicy Yellow Dal (page 182). Or serve it as a side dish with any meal.

Serves 6

2	cups basmati rice
3–4	tablespoons canola oil
2	cinnamon sticks
6	whole cloves
3	bay leaves
5	cardamom pods
1½	teaspoons cumin seeds
3	cups water
¾	teaspoon salt
½	cup fresh or thawed frozen peas
½	teaspoon saffron, or to taste

Rinse the rice three or four times in cold water, to rinse off the starch; let it soak for 5 to 10 minutes. Measure the canola oil into a large saucepan. Add the cinnamon, cloves, bay leaves, cardamom and cumin. Cook over low heat for 2 minutes. Add the water, rice, salt and green peas. Bring to a boil, then cook, covered over medium heat until the water has been absorbed. Add the saffron, and reduce the heat to low. Cover the pan with a clean dishtowel and lid. Cook for an additional 5 minutes, then remove from the heat, keeping the pan covered for 10 minutes. Fluff the rice with a fork, and serve.

Indian Saffron Rice

Chef Sid Andersen
Presenter at Vegfest
Masala Maza Foods
www.masalamaza.com

This rice uses saffron as a flavoring, but pairs it with sweet raisins and crunchy cashews. It makes any meal taste special. Try it with Chickpea Curry (page 177) or Pumpkin Curry (page 181).

Serves 6

1 cup basmati rice
½ teaspoon sea salt
1 teaspoon expeller pressed canola oil
1 pinch saffron *(see below)*
2 cloves
2 cardamom pods
3 tablespoons golden raisins
¼ cup cashews

Combine the rice, salt, oil and 2½ cups water in a medium saucepan and bring to a boil over high heat. Add the saffron, cloves, and cardamom, cover, lower the heat and cook for 10 minutes. Add the raisins and cashews, cover again, and continue cooking until the rice is tender and has entirely absorbed the water. Fluff the cooked rice with a fork.

___

Saffron
The threads of saffron are dried stigmas from a type of crocus; each flower only produces three, which is part of the reason this spice is so expensive. But despite its reputation as exotic and costly, saffron is actually a good value, because just a few threads can perfume an entire dish with their distinctive, delicate aroma and flavor. In fact, too much saffron can produce a bitter taste. Saffron has an affinity for rice and is also used in creamy sauces and some baked goods. For best quality, buy threads rather than powder. The threads should be bright red. To get the most from your purchase, soak the saffron in a little warm water if adding it to dry foods, and add it late in the cooking process so excessive heat doesn't fade the flavor.

Thai Tofu *Thailand*

Nearly Normal's
109 NW 15th Street, Corvallis, OR (541) 753-0791

The tofu in this dish is imbued with the bright flavors of lemongrass and ginger. Note that a wide range of chile peppers called for, so you can adjust the spice level from mildly tingly to wildly hot. Serve this dish over rice.

Serves 4

	Vegetable oil	1	large onion, sliced
1	package (14–16 ounces) firm tofu	8	ounces white mushrooms, sliced
4–5	stalks lemongrass, trimmed *(see page 206)*	1	(14-ounce) can coconut milk
		1	(14-ounce) can baby corn
3	medium cloves garlic	4	ounces snow peas
1½	tablespoons grated fresh ginger	5–15	whole dried red chile peppers (to taste)
¼	cup tamari		
¼	cup nonalcoholic white wine	1	cup fresh basil leaves, chopped coarse

Preheat the oven to 350°F. Generously oil a rimmed baking sheet. Cut the block of tofu into roughly ½-inch thick slices, and cut each slice in half diagonally to make two triangles. Place the tofu triangles on the prepared baking sheet, and bake for 20 to 30 minutes, turning once.

While the tofu is baking, bring 1½ cups water to a boil in a small saucepan, toss the lemongrass into the boiling water, boil for one minute, remove from heat and steep for 5 minutes. Strain the water and reserve, discarding the lemongrass. In a blender, mix the garlic, ginger, tamari, wine and lemongrass "tea." Remove the tofu from the oven, and pour the liquid mixture over it as a marinade.

In a large skillet, sauté the onion in 2 tablespoons of oil over medium heat until translucent. Add the sliced mushrooms, tofu and chile peppers. Reserve the marinade. Sauté until the mushrooms have turned color and lost their moisture. Add the tofu marinade, the coconut milk and baby corn. When the sauce bubbles, add the snow peas, and continue to sauté for 2 to 3 minutes, until the peas turn bright green. Add the basil and serve.

Bahn Thai Tofu in Peanut sauce *Thailand*

Bahn Thai
409 Roy Street, Seattle, WA (206) 283-0444

In this rich and savory dish sautéed fresh spinach is topped with fried tofu and peanut sauce.

Serves 4

1   (14-ounce) can coconut milk
1   teaspoon curry powder
1   teaspoon red chili paste
½   teaspoon sugar
1   teaspoon soy sauce
⅔   cup crunchy peanut butter, plus more
     if necessary

1   tablespoon canola oil
1   package (14–16 ounces) firm tofu,
     cut into 1-inch dice
1   bunch spinach, washed, stems removed

For the sauce: Combine the coconut milk, curry powder, red chili paste, sugar and soy sauce in a medium saucepan. Bring to a boil and simmer for about 15 minutes. Add the peanut butter and stir until the sauce is thick and creamy. If the sauce seems too thin, you may add a little more peanut butter. Set aside, covered, to keep warm.

Heat the oil in a large nonstick skillet over medium heat. Add the tofu and sauté until the edges are brown and crispy, about 2 minutes on each side. Toss in the spinach and allow it to wilt. Transfer the tofu and spinach to a serving dish and pour the peanut sauce over it.

Vegetarian Pad Thai *Thailand*

Bai Tong
15859 Pacific Highway S, Seatac, WA (206) 431-0893

A classic dish, perhaps the most famous Thai meal. Have all the ingredients ready near the stove and the cooking will go very quickly.

Serves 2

6 tablespoons vegetable oil	2 tablespoons tamarind juice or lime juice
1 small shallot, chopped fine	1 tablespoon ketchup
12 ounces fresh narrow rice noodles	2 tablespoons sugar
4 ounces firm tofu, diced small	½ teaspoon salt
3 tablespoons pickled white radish, chopped	2 cups bean sprouts
3 tablespoons ground roasted peanuts	6–7 scallions, white and green parts, cut into 1-inch lengths
1 tablespoon ground dried chile peppers	

Heat 3 tablespoons of the oil in a large frying pan over medium-high heat, add the shallots and sauté until browned. Add the noodles to the pan and fry, stirring constantly, for 1 to 2 minutes. Move the noodles to the sides of the pan and add the remaining 3 tablespoons oil to the center.

When the oil is hot, add the tofu, pickled white radish, peanuts, chiles, tamarind juice, ketchup, sugar, salt and ½ cup of the bean sprouts to the center of the pan and stir to mix thoroughly. Stir the noodles into the mixture and fry, stirring, for 3 minutes. Serve with the scallions and remaining bean sprouts on the side.

Thai Tofu Pumpkin Curry Thailand

Ashland Food Co-op

237 N 1st Street, Ashland, OR (541) 482-2237
www.ashlandfood.coop

This recipe may seem a bit labor-intensive, but the results are oh-so rewarding. The colors are appealing to both eye and palate and the silky, slightly piquant sauce makes a wonderful topping for jasmine or brown basmati rice. The tofu marinade recipe is an added bonus. We use it for our wildly popular baked tofu. Just ladle it over the tofu and bake it until the marinade has been absorbed and the tofu is springy, but not too soft to the touch…Ashland Food Co-op

Serves 4

1	package (14 –16 ounces) firm tofu	6	ounces yellow squash, cut into ½-inch rounds or wedges
3	cups Tofu Marinade *(see recipe below)*	1½	teaspoons red curry paste
¼	cup fresh basil leaves, coarsely chopped	1	(15-ounce) can pumpkin puree
1½	tablespoons toasted sesame oil	1	(14-ounce) can coconut milk
1	yellow onion (about ½ pound), sliced in crescents	1	tablespoon lime juice
6	ounces green beans, trimmed and halved	½–1	teaspoon salt, to taste
6	ounces green cabbage, cut into large chunks	1	scallion, cut on the diagonal in ½-inch pieces

Heat the oven to 375°F. Cut the tofu into rectangles approximately 1 inch long by ½ inch deep and ½ inch wide. Lay the tofu pieces in a single layer in a 9 by 13-inch baking dish and pour the marinade evenly over them. Sprinkle 2 tablespoons of the basil over the tofu. Cover the dish with foil and bake for 40 minutes. Turn the tofu then bake, uncovered, for an additional 15 minutes, or until the tofu is semi-firm and the marinade has soaked in.

While the tofu is baking, heat the sesame oil in a large skillet over medium heat. Add the onion and sauté for 5 minutes. Add the green beans, cabbage and squash and sauté for an additional 5 minutes. Sprinkle in the remaining 2 tablespoons of basil and stir. Immediately add the curry paste and stir until dissolved, then add the pumpkin, coconut milk and baked tofu and stir to mix the ingredients thoroughly. Add the lime juice and salt. Simmer until the vegetables are al dente. Garnish with the scallion pieces, and serve.

Tofu Marinade

This recipe makes 6 cups, which is more than you'll need for the tofu curry recipe above. However it stores well in the refrigerator for up to two months.

2	cups hot water
1¼	cups brown rice syrup
1¼	cups vegan Worcestershire sauce
1¼	cups shoyu (Japanese soy sauce)
2	teaspoons garlic granules
2	teaspoons onion powder
4	teaspoons dried chervil
¾	teaspoon Spike seasoning *(see below)*
1	teaspoon black pepper

Mix all ingredients well with a whisk.

Spike Seasoning
Spike seasoning is a special blend of 39 herbs, spices and vegetables that is made both with and without salt. It is available at many natural food stores.

Spicy Tofu with Mushrooms and Eggplant *Thailand*

Chantanee Family Thai Restaurant
150 105th Avenue NE, Bellevue, WA (425) 455 3226
www.chantanee.com

This delicious curry is a signature dish at Chantanee and its sister restaurant Pen Thai. They use Mae Ploy brand red curry paste and coconut milk. Asian eggplants are long and narrow.

Serves 4

- 1 package (14–16 ounces) firm tofu, cut into 1-inch cubes
- 3 tablespoons canola oil
- 1 tablespoon red curry paste
- 1 (14-ounce) can coconut milk
- 8 ounces white mushrooms, diced (about 2 cups)

- 1 pound Asian eggplants, diced (about 2 cups)
- 3 cups vegetable broth
- 1 tablespoon sugar
- 1 tablespoon soy sauce
- 1 small bunch basil leaves

Boil or steam the tofu until heated through, about 2 minutes, then set aside on a large platter and cover to keep warm. (Alternatively the tofu may be fried in a small amount of canola oil, a few minutes on each side until browned. A nonstick skillet works best for this.) Heat a large skillet over low heat and add the oil and red curry paste; stir to mix the two together until you can smell the curry aroma. Pour the coconut milk into the paste and stir to mix. Turn the heat to medium high, add the mushrooms and eggplant, and cook for 2 minutes. Add the vegetable broth, sugar and soy sauce, and continue to cook until the vegetables are tender. Add the basil leaves, stir just until wilted, and pour onto prepared tofu. Serve immediately.

Garlic Vegetables Thailand

Pen Thai Restaurant

10107 Main Street, Bothell, WA (425) 398-7300
www.chantanee.com

Pen Thai is the sister restaurant to Chantanee. Both restaurants use similar recipes. This colorful side dish is quick and easy to make.

Serves 4

6 tablespoons soy sauce
3 tablespoons chili paste
1 tablespoon sugar
6 cloves garlic
1 small bunch cilantro
½ teaspoon black pepper
3 tablespoons canola oil
1 small bunch broccoli (about 1 pound),
     cut in bite-size pieces

1 (14-ounce) can baby corn, drained and
     halved lengthwise
8 ounces snow peas, trimmed
3 medium carrots, peeled and cut in
     thin matchsticks
2 small zucchini, cut in thin matchsticks
1 cup water

Whisk together the soy sauce, chili paste and sugar in a small bowl and set aside. Place the garlic, cilantro and black pepper in a food processor and pulse until very finely minced. Heat a wok over medium heat and add the oil and blended garlic, cilantro and black pepper. Cook, stirring, until the garlic turns golden brown. Add the broccoli, corn, snow peas, carrots and zucchini, and stir-fry until the vegetables are crisp-tender. Add the soy sauce mixture and water, simmer briefly, and serve immediately.

Hot and Sour Veggies *Thailand*

Thai on Alki

1325 Harbor Avenue SW, Seattle, WA (206) 938-2992

This vegetable dish is low in fat but high in flavor. Roasted curry paste is available in Asian markets. If you can't find it, you can use the more readily available red curry paste, which is sold in the international aisle of many supermarkets.

Serves 4

1   small bunch broccoli (about 1 pound), stalks peeled, stalks and florets cut in bite-size pieces
1   medium zucchini, sliced thin
1   pound napa cabbage, sliced thin
1   pound green cabbage, sliced thin
2   medium carrots, sliced thin
1   medium onion, sliced thin

1   (14-ounce) can baby corn, cut lengthwise
1   tablespoon salt
6   tablespoons sugar
¾   cup lime juice
3   tablespoons roasted curry paste
4   scallions, sliced

Fill a large saucepan with water and bring it to a boil. Add the broccoli, zucchini, napa cabbage, cabbage, carrots, onion and baby corn to the boiling water. Add the salt, sugar, lime juice and roasted curry paste to the boiling vegetables. Boil for a few minutes, until the vegetables are tender, then drain. Garnish with the sliced scallions.

Ginger Asparagus *Thailand*

Tawon Thai

3410 Fremont Ave N, Seattle, WA (206) 633-4545
www.tawonthai.com

The fresh taste of asparagus provides the bass note in this medley of vegetables.

Serves 4

2 medium cloves garlic, chopped (about 2 teaspoons)	12 white mushrooms, sliced
1 tablespoon canola oil	1 small red bell pepper, sliced
1 pound asparagus, tough ends trimmed, cut on the diagonal in 1-inch pieces	1 small green bell pepper, sliced
4 scallions, white parts only, sliced thin	1 tablespoon grated fresh ginger
1 small onion, sliced	1 teaspoon black bean garlic sauce
2 medium celery ribs, sliced	1 tablespoon sugar
2 medium carrots, peeled and cut crosswise	1 teaspoon low-sodium soy sauce

Heat the oil in a medium skillet over medium heat, add the garlic and cook, stirring until the garlic turns brown. Add all the vegetables, the ginger and the black bean garlic sauce, and stir-fry until the vegetables are crisp-tender, about 3 minutes. Season with the sugar and soy sauce and serve.

Vegetable Curry *Thailand*

Thai Kitchen of Bellevue
14116 NE 20th Street, Bellevue, WA (425) 641-9166

This is the perfect winter stew, Thai-style. Sautéing the curry paste with the thick cream from the coconut milk helps to intensify the curry flavor and distribute it evenly.

Serves 4

¼ cup vegetable oil
2 (14-ounce) cans coconut milk
⅓ cup yellow curry paste
1 cup water
1 pound waxy potatoes, peeled and diced small
2 medium carrots, sliced
1 pound green cabbage, cut into bite-size pieces
1 medium bunch broccoli (about 1½ pounds), cut into bite-size pieces

1 (14-ounce) can baby corn
1 small red bell pepper, sliced
1 small green bell pepper, sliced
1 medium zucchini, sliced crosswise ½ inch thick
8 ounces white mushrooms, sliced
1 small onion, diced
1 teaspoon salt
1 teaspoon sugar

Heat the oil in a large saucepan or Dutch oven over medium heat. Open the cans of coconut milk, skim the thick cream from the top of both cans, and add it to the pan along with the curry paste. Sauté until the cream thickens. Add the remaining coconut milk and the water and stir. Add the potatoes and carrots and simmer for 10 minutes, then add the remaining vegetables. Stir until mixed well. Bring to a boil, then cover and simmer until the vegetables are crisp-tender. Add the salt and sugar and stir until mixed well. Remove from heat and serve.

Stir Fried Tempeh *Chinese*

China Gorge Restaurant

2680 Old Columbia River Drive, Hood River, OR (541) 386-5331
www.chinagorge.com

The robust flavor of tempeh adds a twist to this stir-fry. Mushroom soy sauce is Chinese soy sauce blended with Chinese black mushrooms. It is sold in Asian markets.

Serves 4

1 tablespoon cornstarch	½ medium red bell pepper, diced
4 tablespoons water	½ medium green bell pepper, diced
4 tablespoons soybean oil	1 (5-ounce) can water chestnuts, drained and diced
2 (8-ounce) packages tempeh, cut into cubes	4 ounces button mushrooms, halved or quartered, depending on size
4 cloves garlic, chopped	2 scallions, cut into 1½-inch pieces
4 tablespoons mushroom soy sauce	1 small white onion, diced
2 tablespoons soy sauce	1 tablespoon toasted sesame oil
Hot chili paste	

In a small bowl, whisk together the cornstarch and 2 tablespoons of the water; set aside. Heat 2 tablespoons of the oil in a large skillet or wok over medium-high heat, add the tempeh cubes, and stir-fry, turning the pieces, until browned on all sides, about 8 minutes.

Remove the tempeh from the pan, add the remaining 2 tablespoons of oil and the garlic and sauté until the garlic is light golden brown, about 5 minutes. Add the remaining 2 tablespoons water, both soy sauces, and chili paste to taste, and stir. Add the red and green peppers, the water chestnuts, mushrooms, onion and scallions, and stir-fry until the vegetables are crisp-tender. Add the cornstarch/water mixture, then the tempeh, and stir-fry until the sauce is thickened and the tempeh is heated through. Drizzle the sesame oil over the dish and serve.

Chef's Tip

To remove any "tinny" flavor from canned water chestnuts, blanch them briefly in boiling water, then dip them in ice water until cool, and drain them.

Tofu Rolls with Spicy Tomato Sauce Chinese

The Teapot Vegetarian House,
125 15th Avenue E, Seattle, WA (206) 325-1010

This is a popular dish at the Teapot Vegetarian House. Its appeal lies in the crunchiness of the tofu roll, the soft yielding tofu filling, and the zesty tomato sauce. You may spice up this sauce by adding a spoonful of chili paste. Wood ear mushrooms (also called black fungus) are a Chinese delicacy, available at Asian markets. You can substitute thinly sliced shiitake mushrooms.

Serves 4

Tofu roll
- 1 package (14 –16 ounces) firm tofu
- 2 teaspoons salt
- 2 teaspoons sugar
- 4 tablespoons chopped wood ear mushrooms
- 1 medium carrot, diced
- ½ cup peas
- 2 sheets tofu skin *(see facing page)*
- 8 cups oil for frying, such as peanut
- 2 cup all purpose white flour
- 4 cups water

Sauce
- 2 tablespoons vegetable oil
- 2 cloves garlic, minced
- 8 white button mushrooms, sliced
- 1 medium carrot, diced
- ½ cup peas
- 2 cups tomato sauce
- 1 cup sugar
- 2 tablespoons black soy sauce
-    Hot chili paste (optional)
- 1 tablespoon toasted sesame oil

To make the tofu rolls, crumble the tofu with a fork and mix in the salt, sugar, wood ear, carrot and peas. Cut the tofu skins in half. Working with 1 piece at a time, place the tofu skin on the work surface with a short side facing you. Spoon one fourth of the filling mixture across the lower third of the tofu skin. Fold the bottom of the skin up over the filling, tuck in the sides, and continue to roll up, as for a spring roll.

Heat the oil in a deep pot to 375°F. While the oil is heating, place the flour in a medium bowl, add the water, and whisk to blend. Dip each tofu roll into the batter until fully coated. Dip the battered tofu rolls into the hot oil and fry until crisp and golden brown. Remove the rolls from the oil, slice each one in half, and place the pieces on a serving dish.

To make the sauce, heat the oil in a medium saucepan over medium-high heat, add the garlic, and sauté until light golden brown. Add the mushrooms and carrots and sauté until the vegetables are softened, then add the peas, tomato sauce, sugar, soy sauce and chili paste to taste, if using, and stir well. Let simmer for 5 minutes, then ladle the sauce over the sliced tofu rolls, sprinkle with the sesame oil, and serve.

Tofu Skin

Tofu skins, or bean curd sheets, are large dried sheets made from the skin that forms on the surface of soymilk when it is heated. They may be soaked before using or, if being used in a crispy dish, left as is. Look for bean curd sheets in Asian markets, where they may be found in the freezer section.

Bryanna's Sizzling Tofu and Mushroom Stew Chinese

Chef Bryanna Clark Grogan
Author, Presenter at Vegfest
Recipe from *Authentic Chinese Cuisine for the Contemporary Kitchen: All Vegan Recipes,*
published by Book Publishing Company
www.bryannaclarkgrogan.com

This recipe was presented at Vegfest. It is a very quick and easy Chinese hotpot dish, containing ingredients many of us have around all the time. Serve over rice.

Serves 3 to 4

2	tablespoons light soy sauce	1	tablespoon water
2	tablespoons nonalcoholic cooking sherry	2	tablespoons vegetable oil
½	tablespoon roasted sesame oil	2	cloves garlic, minced
2½	teaspoons cornstarch	1	medium onion, sliced thin
1	teaspoon minced ginger	4	large white mushrooms, sliced
½	teaspoon sugar	¼	cup frozen baby peas
	Dash white pepper	1	cup vegetable broth
10	ounces extra-firm tofu, cut into ¾-inch cubes	2	scallions, chopped

In a medium bowl, whisk together the 1 tablespoon of the soy sauce, 1 tablespoon of the sherry, the sesame oil, 1 teaspoon of the cornstarch, the ginger, sugar and pepper. Add the tofu cubes, stir to coat, and marinate at least 20 minutes. In a small bowl, whisk together the remaining soy sauce, sherry and cornstarch with the water and set aside.

Heat a large wok or heavy frying pan over high heat. Add 1 tablespoon of the oil. When the oil is hot, add the tofu and the marinade. Stir-fry until the marinade is absorbed and the cubes are glazed. Remove the tofu from the pan.

In the same pan, heat the remaining tablespoon of oil over high heat. When the oil is hot, add the garlic and onion and stir-fry until the onion wilts. Add the mushrooms, peas, tofu cubes and broth. Bring to a boil and then simmer, covered, for about 3 minutes. Stir in the reserved cornstarch mixture. Stir until the broth has thickened. Sprinkle with the scallions and serve hot.

Reprinted with permission

Bryanna's Spicy Sichuan Eggplant Chinese

Chef Bryanna Clark Grogan

Author, Presenter at Vegfest
Recipe from *Authentic Chinese Cuisine for the Contemporary Kitchen: All Vegan Recipes*,
published by Book Publishing Company
www.bryannaclarkgrogan.com

This delicious eggplant dish eliminates the deep-frying, but not the flavor. If you can't find the small Asian eggplants, use the large Western variety, but peel them. If the eggplant is less than perfectly fresh (smooth and shiny), salt the strips and let them drain in a colander for 30 minutes, then rinse them off well and dry them before cooking.

Serves 4

- 1 cup vegetable broth
- 2 tablespoons light soy sauce
- 2 tablespoons rice, cider or white wine vinegar
- 1 tablespoon nonalcoholic cooking sherry
- 1 tablespoon chili garlic paste
- 1 teaspoon sugar
- 1 scallion, chopped fine

- 2 pounds small Asian eggplants, cut into strips about ¾-inch thick
- 2 teaspoons vegetable oil
- 3 cloves garlic, minced
- 2 tablespoons minced fresh ginger
- 2 teaspoons cornstarch dissolved in
- 2 tablespoons cold water

To make the cooking sauce, whisk together the broth, soy sauce, vinegar, sherry, chili garlic paste, sugar and scallion in a medium bowl. Set aside.

Preheat the broiler. Place the eggplant strips on nonstick or lightly greased baking sheets. Broil 3 to 4 inches from the heat until browned; turn over and brown the other side. The insides should be soft. Set aside.

Heat a large skillet or wok over high heat, add the oil, and heat until shimmering. Add the garlic and ginger and stir-fry for a few seconds. Add the broiled eggplant strips and the broth mixture. Mix well and cook over high heat for 2 minutes. Add the dissolved cornstarch and cook, stirring, until the sauce has thickened. Serve.

Wendy's Lemongrass Tofu Vietnamese

Wendy's Vietnamese Restaurants

Freighthouse Square, 430 East D Street, Tacoma, WA (253) 572-4678
Wendy's II, 5015 Tacoma Mall Boulevard, Tacoma, WA (253) 471-0228

Wendy uses Yuen Vegetarian Seasoning, available at Asian markets, in this dish. You may substitute Spike or any other brand of vegetable-and-herb seasoning blend.

Serves 4

4	tablespoons vegetable oil	2	teaspoons sugar
1	medium yellow onion, sliced		Ground black pepper
4	cloves garlic, chopped	½	cup water
4	stalks lemongrass, chopped *(see below)*	1	medium cucumber, peeled and sliced thin
1	package (14–16 ounces) firm tofu, cubed	16	large leaves lettuce, shredded
1	tablespoon vegetarian seasoning	4	scallions, white and light green parts, chopped

Heat a large skillet or wok over high heat. Add the oil, onion, garlic and lemongrass, and stir-fry until light golden brown. Add the tofu, vegetarian seasoning, sugar and pepper, if desired. Pour in the water, stir briefly, cover, reduce the heat to low, and simmer 10 minutes.

To serve, place some shredded lettuce on the bottom of each plate. Spoon a portion of the tofu over the lettuce, then place some cucumber slices around the tofu. Sprinkle some scallion pieces on top of the tofu and serve. Place cucumbers around the lettuce and pour the tofu over the lettuce.

Lemongrass
Lemongrass is a citrusy herb that slightly resembles a long, woody scallion. Fresh lemongrass is sold in bundles in Asian markets and some well-stocked supermarkets. It is usually trimmed at the bulb end and the top inch or two is discarded. Only about 3 inches at the bulb end is used for cooking. It may be smashed and used to infuse broths and stews with flavor, or it may be finely chopped.

Wendy's Tofu Noodles *Vietnamese*

Wendy's Vietnamese Restaurants

Freighthouse Square, 430 East D Street, Tacoma, WA (253) 572-4678
Wendy's II, 5015 Tacoma Mall Boulevard, Tacoma, WA (253) 471-0228

This dish is assembled in layers. Guests can toss the ingredients together to blend the flavors. Wendy uses Yuen Vegetarian Seasoning, available at Asian markets, in this dish. You may substitute Spike or any other brand of vegetable-and-herb seasoning blend.

Serves 4

16 ounces rice noodles	1 small head lettuce, thinly sliced
4 tablespoons vegetable oil	4 ounces bean sprouts
1 medium yellow onion, sliced	1 cucumber, peeled and diced
1 package (14 –16 ounces) tofu, diced small	1 carrot, shredded
Ground black pepper	¼ cup chopped peanuts
4 tablespoons vegetarian seasoning	2 tablespoons minced fresh parsley
½ cup rice vinegar	

In a large saucepan, bring 8 cups of water to a boil over high heat, add the noodles, and cook for 5 minutes. Strain and rinse in hot water; leave the noodles in the colander so they can drain thoroughly.

Heat a wok or large skillet over high heat and add 2 tablespoons of the oil. Add the onion and stir-fry until brown, then add the tofu and a pinch of black pepper. Add the vegetarian seasoning, cover, reduce heat and simmer for 10 minutes.

On individual dishes, make a bed of the sliced lettuce, then add the bean sprouts and diced cucumber, and top with the cooked noodles. Spoon the tofu over the noodles and top with the shredded carrots. Whisk the vinegar with the remaining 2 tablespoons of oil and pour over the carrots, then garnish with the chopped peanuts and parsley.

Vietnamese Rice Noodles with Veggies and Tofu

Zao Noodle Bar
2630 NE University Village Street, Seattle, WA (206) 529-8278

Although the ingredient list for this dish is long, once you have the ingredients prepared, the dish is very quick to put together. This is a fun meal to make for guests; each person receives a large bowl with layers of components that they can toss. Sambal oelek is an Asian condiment made of hot chiles.

Dressing
- ½ cup sugar
- 1 cup water
- 6 tablespoons soy sauce
- 2 tablespoons fresh lime juice (from 1 lime)
- 1 teaspoon sambal oelek
- 1 clove garlic, minced or pressed through a garlic press

Noodles, Veggies and Tofu
- 2 tablespoons chopped fresh ginger
- 3 cloves garlic, halved
- 1 stalk lemongrass, chopped *(see page 206)*
- 2 tablespoons chopped fresh mint
- 2 tablespoons chopped fresh Thai basil
- 2 tablespoons chopped fresh Vietnamese coriander *(see facing page)*
- 4 ounces bean sprouts
- 1 small cucumber, peeled, seeded, and cut in thin, 2-inch strips

- 1 small head red leaf lettuce, chopped
- 16 ounces rice vermicelli, cooked
- 1 cup canola oil
- 4 medium shallots, sliced
- 8 ounces extra-firm tofu, diced
- 2 cups small broccoli florets, blanched
- ¼ head green cabbage, shredded
- 3 medium carrots, 2 cut in thin, 2-inch strips and 1 shredded
- 1 medium zucchini, cut in thin, 2-inch strips
- 1 medium yellow squash, cut in thin, 2-inch strips
- 4 tablespoons soy sauce
- 4 tablespoons finely chopped peanuts Cilantro sprigs, for garnish
- 4 tablespoons sambal oelek

To make the dressing, put the sugar in a medium bowl, add 1 cup water and whisk until the sugar is dissolved. Add the soy sauce, lime juice, sambal oelek and garlic, and whisk to blend. Set aside.

Place the ginger, garlic and lemongrass in a food processor or mini-chopper and pulse until they are finely minced (or you may use a mortar and pestle to crush them). Set aside near the stove.

Divide the mint, basil and Vietnamese coriander evenly among 4 large soup or pasta bowls. Add the bean sprouts, cucumber and lettuce. Finally divide the rice noodles among the bowls, spreading it to cover the other ingredients.

Heat 2 tablespoons of the canola oil in a large skillet over medium-high heat. Add half of the shallots and sauté until they are crisp and golden brown. Lift the shallots from the pan and set on a paper-towel-lined plate. Return the pan to the heat, add the remaining 6 tablespoons of oil, add the tofu and stir-fry until the tofu is lightly browned on all sides, about 8 minutes. Add the ginger-garlic-lemongrass mix and stir-fry until fragrant, about 30 seconds. Add the broccoli, cabbage, 2 sliced carrots, zucchini and yellow squash to the pan and stir-fry for 2 minutes. Add the soy sauce, stir to coat the vegetables, and remove the pan from the heat.

Spoon some of the vegetables and tofu on top of the rice noodles in each bowl, and then pour the dressing over the top. Garnish with the chopped peanuts, fried shallots, grated carrot, cilantro sprigs and a dollop of sambal oelek, passing the remaining sambal oelek at the table. Encourage guests to thoroughly mix the contents of their bowls: Mixing the dressing that has settled on the bottom with the sambal on the top will even out the spiciness. Mixing the herbs from the bottom of the bowl well with the other ingredients will give the dish the proper flavor.

Vietnamese Coriander

Vietnamese coriander, also known as rau ram, has a coriander-like smell with a clear lemony note. It is available at some Asian markets and is best used fresh. If you cannot find it, you may increase the amount of mint or basil to suit your taste.

Soba Noodles and Vegetables *Yaki-Soba, Japanese*

Chef Kati Peters
Presenter at Vegfest
Seattle, WA
www.chefkati.com

Soba noodles are made with buckwheat, which gives them a wonderfully hearty flavor. If you prefer, you can use dried shiitake mushrooms in this recipe; soak them in hot water for 20 minutes to reconstitute them. Usu-age, or deep fried tofu, is available packaged at Asian markets.

Serves 4

1   (10-ounce) package dried soba noodles
3   tablespoons vegetable oil (up to half can be toasted sesame oil)
1   onion, sliced
2   cloves garlic, crushed
1   large carrot, sliced thin
1   red bell pepper, sliced thin

1   zucchini, sliced thin
4   ounces shiitake mushrooms, stems discarded, caps sliced thin
1–2 pieces usu-age (deep fried tofu), sliced
1   tablespoon nonalcoholic mirin (Japanese rice wine)
2–3 tablespoons shoyu (Japanese soy sauce)
    Salt and freshly ground black pepper

Cook the noodles as the package directs, making sure not to overcook them. Heat a wok or large frying pan and coat with oil. Add the onion and garlic and sauté until partially cooked. Then add the carrot, pepper, zucchini, mushrooms and usu-age, mixing well. Add the shoyu and mirin and simmer a few minutes until the veggies are crisp-tender. Add the cooked noodles, rinsing with hot tap water first if they have gotten stuck together. Shake off excess water. Keep tossing to marry the flavors.

Udon with Vegetables and Mochi *Japanese*

Chef Kati Peters
Presenter at Vegfest
Seattle, WA
www.chefkati.com

This is easy and so yummy, especially in the winter.

Serves 4

- 1 (3-ounce) package dried udon noodles
- 1 strip konbu seaweed
- 5 shiitake mushrooms, caps only, fresh or dried
- 1 small head napa cabbage, sliced crosswise in 1-inch strips
- 2 large carrots, sliced diagonally
- 2 leeks, sliced diagonally
- 1 large zucchini, sliced diagonally
- White miso *(see below)*
- 1 (12-ounce) package brown rice mochi, cut in 1-inch squares
- Shichimi (a blend of seven spices)

Bring 8 cups of water to a boil in a large saucepan over high heat, add the udon noodles, and cook just until tender. Drain, rinse and set aside. Place the strip of konbu and 8 to 10 cups water in a large soup pot, and bring to a boil. Add the mushrooms, cabbage, carrots, leeks and zucchini and simmer until the carrots are crisp-tender. Reduce the heat to just under a simmer, add the cooked noodles, miso to taste, and mochi squares. After the mochi softens, serve, passing the shichimi at the table for guests to sprinkle on their own portion.

Miso
Miso is a rich, salty condiment that characterizes the essence of Japanese cooking. The Japanese use miso to flavor a variety of foods. It is made from soybeans and sometimes a grain such as rice, combined with salt and a mold culture, and then aged in cedar vats for one to three years. In Japan, different types of miso are prepared and evaluated much the way Westerners judge fine wines and cheeses. Unpasteurized miso contains live cultures and is sold in the refrigerated sections of natural food stores and Asian markets. To preserve its beneficial cultures, don't boil miso.

Udon Noodles with Sesame Tamari Sauce and Kale *Japanese*

Rita Condon BS Nutrition
PCC Cooks Instructor
www.pccnaturalmarkets.com/pcccooks/instructors

The sauce for this noodle dish makes a great dip for fresh vegetables such as slices of red pepper, carrot and celery sticks, radishes, and lightly steamed broccoli and cauliflower. If you'd like to boost the protein in this dish, add a pound of firm tofu that has been cut into ½ inch chunks and sautéed in olive oil until crisp.

Serves 4 to 6

Sauce

- ¾ cup raw tahini
- ¾ cup water
- ½ cup tamari
- 3 tablespoons brown rice vinegar
- 2 tablespoons toasted sesame oil
- 2 medium cloves garlic, minced
  2-inch piece fresh ginger, grated

Noodles

- 2 (8.8-ounce) packages whole-wheat udon noodles
- 1 tablespoon extra virgin olive oil
- 1 large bunch kale, stems removed, leaves chopped
- 6 lemon wedges

Thoroughly combine the sauce ingredients in a bowl and set aside. Cook the udon noodles according to package instructions. Drain, rinse and put into a large pasta bowl.

Heat the olive oil over medium heat in a large skillet. Add the chopped kale in large handfuls, allowing the kale to wilt slightly before adding the next handful. Sauté the kale until done, about 5 to 8 minutes. Remove from heat and add to the udon noodles. Pour the sesame tamari sauce over the noodles and toss until well combined. Serve with a lemon wedge to squeeze over the top.

Kinpira *Japanese*

Chef Karen Martin
Presenter at Vegfest
macromama@msn.com

The name of this dish, presented at Vegfest, actually describes the cooking method used for it. It means "sauté and simmer." Strengthening and nourishing, this dish combines three sweet, crunchy root vegetables; carrot, burdock and lotus root. Burdock and lotus root are sold in Asian markets.

Serves 2

1	teaspoon dark or light sesame oil
8	ounces burdock, cut into very fine matchsticks
	Pinch of sea salt
8	ounces lotus root, cut into very fine matchsticks *(see below)*
2	medium carrots, cut into very fine matchsticks
	Spring or filtered water
	Shoyu (Japanese soy sauce)
	Freshly squeezed ginger juice (optional)

Heat a heavy skillet over medium-high heat. Add the sesame oil, burdock, and a pinch of sea salt, stir to coat the burdock with the oil, and cook for about 2 minutes. Spread the burdock evenly over the skillet bottom, then layer the lotus root evenly and finally the carrots. Do not stir!

Add water to just cover the burdock, season lightly with soy sauce and cover. Reduce the heat to medium-low and cook for 10 minutes. Remove the lid and simmer until all the liquid has evaporated or been absorbed, about 20 minutes. Drizzle fresh ginger juice to taste, if using, over the vegetables during the last 5 minutes of cooking.

Lotus Root
The root of the lotus flower is a long, segmented vegetable that is starchy, mildly sweet, and crunchy, a little like jicama. Rather homely on the outside, when cut crosswise, it reveals a beautiful daisy pattern of holes. Lotus root may be sold whole with mud still clinging to it; look for firm, unblemished roots. Once peeled, it discolors quickly; if you're not using it immediately, place cut pieces in cold water with a splash of lemon juice. Lotus root is wonderful in salads and soups. It can also be pickled, stir-fried, stuffed and steamed.

Desserts

Orange Blackberry Cake American

Swan Café
1220 N Forest, Bellingham, WA (360) 734-8158
www.communityfood.coop

This is a delightfully refreshing cake, with the winning combination of citrus and fresh berries. Try it with your favorite berries—raspberries, salmonberries, marionberries, blueberries—or a mixture.

Makes one 9-inch cake

6	cups unbleached white flour	1	tablespoon vanilla
4½	cups plus ⅓ cup granulated sugar	6	cups blackberries
4	teaspoons baking soda	⅓	cup cane sugar
2	teaspoons sea salt	3	tablespoons corn starch
1	cup canola oil	2	cups powdered sugar
½	cup grated zest and 3 cups juice from 6 medium oranges, preferably organic		

To make the cake, heat the oven to 350°F (325 if using a convection oven). Grease three 9-inch round cake pans, line the bottoms with waxed paper, and grease and flour the paper. Sift the flour, 4½ cups granulated sugar, baking soda and salt into a large bowl. In a separate bowl, combine the canola oil, orange zest and juice, vanilla and 3 cups filtered water, then pour them into the dry ingredients and whisk to combine. Divide the batter evenly into the 3 pans and bake until the layers are golden brown and spring back when touched lightly in the center, 20 to 25 minutes. Cool the layers for 10 minutes in their pans, then turn out onto wire racks and cool completely.

To make the filling, put the blackberries and ⅓ cup sugar in a saucepan and bring them to a boil. Combine the cornstarch with ¼ cup filtered water and stir to dissolve. Add to the berry mixture and simmer for a couple of minutes, then set aside to cool.

To assemble the cake, whisk the powdered sugar with ¼ cup water to make a glaze. Place one cake layer on a plate and spread with ⅓ of the filling, then drizzle with a little of the glaze. Repeat with the second and third cake layers, drizzling any remaining glaze around the edges of the cake so it flows down the sides. Chill to set.

Vegan German Chocolate Cake German

Swan Café

1220 N Forest, Bellingham, WA (360) 734-8158
www.communityfood.coop

This makes the ultimate chocolate cake, perfect for parties and special occasions.

Makes one 9-inch cake

Cake

3	cups unbleached all-purpose flour
2¼	cups granulated sugar
1½	cups cocoa powder
2	teaspoons baking soda
1	teaspoon sea salt
2¼	cups filtered water
1¼	cups canola oil
2	tablespoons apple cider vinegar
2	teaspoons vanilla

Filling

1	cup plain soymilk
2	tablespoons cornstarch
¼	teaspoon sea salt
1½	cup brown sugar
¼	cup soy margarine
3	cups shredded coconut
1½	cups pecans
1	tablespoon vanilla

Ganache

2	tablespoons soy milk
½	cup nondairy semi-sweet chocolate chips

Preheat the oven to 325°F. Grease and flour three 9-inch round cake pans. In a large bowl, sift together the flour, sugar, cocoa powder, baking soda and salt. In a separate bowl, whisk together the water, oil, vinegar and vanilla. Pour the wet ingredients into the dry ingredients and stir to blend. Divide the batter evenly among the prepared pans and bake until the cake tops spring back when pressed lightly, 15 to 20 minutes. Cool for 10 minutes, then turn out of the pans onto wire racks and cool completely.

For the filling, combine the cornstarch, soymilk and salt in a small saucepan and stir to dissolve. Add the brown sugar and margarine. Place the saucepan over medium heat and bring just to a boil, stirring constantly. Remove from the heat, stir in the coconut, pecans and vanilla, and cool.

To make the ganache, place the chocolate and the soymilk in a small saucepan. Warm and stir until the chocolate is melted and the mixture is smooth. Remove from the heat.

Place one cooled cake layer on a dessert platter and top with a third of the coconut mixture, spreading it evenly over the surface and out to the edges (so it will show between the layers). Drizzle a little ganache over the filling. Repeat with the second and third layers, drizzling any remaining ganache over the top.

Vegan Carrot Cake American

Cup & Saucer Café
3566 SE Hawthorne Boulevard, Portland, OR (503) 236-6001

A classic; moist, delectable, and full of healthy goodies. This version uses flour made from spelt, an ancient grain that is similar to wheat but easier to digest.

Makes one 9 by 13-inch cake or one 10-inch Bundt cake

1 cup canola oil	1 cup chopped walnuts, plus more for garnish
1 cup granulated sugar	½ cup raisins (optional)
1 cup brown sugar	
1½ cups soymilk	
4 cups spelt flour	**Frosting**
2 teaspoons baking powder	3 tablespoons canola oil
2 teaspoons baking soda	½ teaspoon vanilla extract
1 teaspoon cinnamon	2 tablespoons maple syrup
½ teaspoon salt	2 cups confectioners' sugar, sifted, plus more if needed
½ teaspoon allspice	
3 cups grated carrots (1 pound)	¼ cup soymilk, plus more if needed

Heat the oven to 345°F. Grease and flour (use spelt flour) a 9 by 13-inch cake pan or a 10-inch Bundt pan. In a large bowl, whisk together the oil, granulated sugar, brown sugar and soymilk. In a medium bowl, whisk together the flour, baking powder, baking soda, cinnamon, salt and allspice. Add the dry ingredient to the wet ingredients and stir thoroughly. Add the carrots, walnuts and raisins, if using, and stir to incorporate. Pour the mixture into the prepared pan and bake until the cake springs back when touched lightly and a toothpick inserted in the center comes out clean, 40 to 60 minutes. Cool the cake on a wire rack and, if using a Bundt pan, invert the cake onto a platter.

To make the frosting, whisk together the oil, vanilla extract and maple syrup. Add the powdered sugar and stir; the mixture will be quite thick. Pour in the soymilk and whisk vigorously. (You may need to add more powdered sugar or soymilk to get the consistency you want; you can either drizzle it or spread it on the cake.) Frost the cooled cake and sprinkle some chopped walnuts over the frosting, if desired.

Chocolate Truffle Pie   *American*

Chef Louise Hagler
Author, Presenter at Vegfest

A little of this rich, fudgy dessert goes a long way. It was very popular at Vegfest. To gild the lily, serve small slices of pie with nondairy whipped topping. Use either a homemade or commercially prepared graham cracker crust for this dessert.

Makes one 8-inch pie (12 servings)

- 1   package (14–16 ounces) firm or extra firm tofu
- ⅔   cup granulated sugar
- 1   teaspoon vanilla, almond, peppermint or coffee extract
- 1   bag (12 ounces) nondairy chocolate chips
- 1   8-inch graham cracker pie shell, baked

In a food processor blend the tofu, sweetener and extract until creamy. Melt the chocolate chips over hot water or in the microwave until they just start to melt, and stir until completely melted, smooth, and creamy. Add the melted chips to the tofu mixture in the food processor and process immediately until creamy. Pour and spread the mixture into the baked pie shell then smooth or shake until evenly distributed in the shell. Chill for at least 4 hours or overnight.

Chef's Tip
To make individual bite size servings, chill the filling until it firms, then scoop with a cookie scoop onto vanilla or ginger wafers and drizzle with melted chocolate. Freeze until ready to serve.

Persian Baklava *Middle Eastern*

Chef Omid Roustaei, MA, ABS

Presenter at Vegfest and chef at Monthly Dining Event
Faculty, School of Natural Cookery in Boulder, Colorado
PCC Cooks Culinary Instructor
www.members.aol.com/wholefoodschef

One (or two) of these sweet treats makes a cup of coffee or tea a special event. Phyllo dough is sold in the freezer case of most supermarkets. To thaw, place the package in the refrigerator the night before you plan to use it.

    4   cups granulated sugar
    1½ cups water
    ½   cup coconut or walnut oil
    ¼   cup rose water
    4   cups almonds
    2   tablespoons ground cardamom
    1   (16-ounce) package phyllo dough, thawed

Preheat the oven to 350°F. Lightly oil a 10 by 15-inch rimmed baking sheet (jelly roll pan) and set aside. In a medium saucepan, combine 2 cups of the sugar, water, and ¼ cup of the coconut oil. Heat over medium-high heat, stirring, until the sugar is dissolved and the mixture is near boiling. Remove from heat, add the rose water, and set aside. Place the almonds, remaining 2 cups of sugar, and cardamom in a food processor, and pulse until the mixture is coarsely ground.

To assemble, remove the phyllo dough from the package, unroll, and cover it with a damp towel to prevent it from drying out as you work. Pour the remaining ¼ cup oil into a small dish for brushing. Lay a sheet of phyllo in the baking sheet and brush it lightly with oil. Repeat until you have a layer of 6 or 7 sheets (you will eventually use all the phyllo sheets; there are about 20 in a package). Spread half of the almond mixture evenly over the top sheet, then layer 6 or 7 more phyllo sheets on top of the nuts, brushing each one lightly with oil. Spread the other half of the almond mixture on the top phyllo sheet, then layer the remaining phyllo sheets in the same manner as the earlier ones.

With a sharp knife, cut the baklava diagonally into 1-inch diamond shapes (be sure to cut all the way through). Pour half of the syrup over the cut baklava and bake until light golden brown, 15 to 20 minutes. Remove from the oven, pour the remaining syrup over the baklava and cool completely. Carefully remove the pieces from the pan and serve.

Pumpkin Spice Blondies *American*

Simple Treats
Seattle, WA (206) 251-8818
www.simpletreats.com

Feel free to use whatever kind of nut you like in these moist squares; pecans, almonds, walnuts, and macadamia nuts are all especially good. Barley flour is ground from pearl barley and is sold at natural food stores. Vegan white chocolate chips are available at pangea-veg.com.

Makes 9 large or 16 medium squares

1¼	cup rolled oats	½	cup plus 2 tablespoons chopped nuts (optional)
¾	cup barley flour		
2	teaspoons cinnamon	¼	cup pumpkin puree
¾	teaspoon baking soda	½	cup canola oil
¾	teaspoon baking powder	½	cup maple syrup
¾	teaspoon salt	¼	cup barley malt syrup
1¼	cups white chocolate chips	½	teaspoon vanilla

Preheat oven to 350°F. Grease a 9 by 9-inch square pan. Place the oats in a food processor and grind them to a coarse but flour-like consistency. Transfer the oat flour into a large bowl, sift the barley flour, baking soda, baking powder and salt into the bowl, and add the white chocolate chips and ½ cup of nuts, if using.

In a small bowl, whisk together the pumpkin puree, canola oil, maple syrup, barley malt and vanilla. Pour the wet ingredients into the dry and mix with a spatula until everything is well incorporated. Pour into a greased baking pan; sprinkle the remaining 2 tablespoons of nuts on top. Bake for 27 minutes. Turn the pan and continue to bake for another 10 to 15 minutes or until golden brown. Let cool for at least 30 minutes before attempting to cut.

Cocoa Halva *Turkish*

Patty Pan Grill
5402 20th Avenue NW, Seattle, WA (206) 782-1558
Chef Devra Gartenstein
Recipe from *The Accidental Vegan,* published by The Crossing Press

A dense, nutty confection. Sesame seeds are high in oil; make sure you purchase fresh ones by buying from a store with rapid turnover.

Makes about 32 pieces

- 1   cup sesame seeds
- ¼   cup tahini
- 2   tablespoons rice syrup
- 1   teaspoon vanilla
- 2   tablespoons cocoa powder

Grind the sesame seeds in a food processor until some of them are powdered, about 3 to 5 minutes. Combine the tahini, rice syrup, vanilla, and cocoa powder in a small saucepan, and heat over low heat, stirring often, until the mixture is liquid and evenly blended. Remove from heat, stir in the sesame seeds, then press the mixture into an 8 by 4-inch loaf pan (or whatever you have available) and cool completely. Cut into 1-inch-square pieces and serve.

Oatmeal Chocolate Chip Cookies *American*

Sam Bond's Garage
407 Blair, Eugene, OR (541) 431-6603

These are big cookies with big flavor. Be sure to leave enough space between the cookies on the sheet so they can spread.

Makes about 36 cookies

2 cups unbleached all-purpose flour	1 cup canola oil
1½ cups whole-wheat pastry flour	½ cup apple juice
1 cup oats	3 tablespoons vanilla
1 teaspoon baking soda	1 cup nondairy chocolate chips
½ teaspoon salt	
2 cups granulated sugar (or 1 cup brown and 1 cup granulated sugar, if you like)	

Preheat the oven to 350°F. Mix both flours, the oats, baking soda and salt in a large bowl and set it aside.

In a medium bowl, whisk together the sugar, canola oil, apple juice and vanilla, and stir in the chocolate chips. Add the wet mixture to the dry ingredients and stir until completely blended. Drop the dough onto a baking sheet, using ¼ cup for each cookie, and flatten to ¾ to 1 inch thick. Bake until golden brown, about 15 to 20 minutes.

Cashew Coconut Date Cookies *American*

Chef Cheryl Redmond
Speaker at Vegfest
Food writer and editor
www.sredmond.com/vt_writing_svcs.htm

You can use pre-ground cardamom for this recipe or grind your own, which will give it a more intense flavor. Break the pods open and crush the black seeds with a mortar and pestle. Be sure the dates you use for this recipe are fresh and moist. Organic medjool dates are particularly nice.

Makes about 40 cookies

1½ cups quick or old-fashioned oats, ground fine in a food processor, or oat flour
1 cup unbleached all-purpose flour
¾ teaspoon sea salt
½ teaspoon baking powder
½ teaspoon baking soda
½ teaspoon ground cardamom
1 cup natural unsalted cashew butter
3 tablespoons water

½ cup maple syrup
1 teaspoon vanilla extract
1 cup natural granulated sugar (like Sucanat)
⅔ cup nonhydrogenated margarine
⅔ cup unsweetened grated coconut
½ cup finely chopped pitted dates
Approximately 40 cashew halves (optional)

Heat the oven to 350°F. Line two baking sheets with parchment paper. In a small bowl whisk together the ground oats, flour, salt, baking powder, baking soda and cardamom; set aside. Using an electric mixer, beat the cashew butter with the water in a large bowl until smooth. Add the maple syrup and vanilla and beat until well blended. Add the sugar and margarine and beat until completely incorporated. Add the dry ingredients and beat on low speed just until completely blended. Stir in the coconut and dates.

Drop the dough by rounded teaspoonfuls onto the baking sheets. Press each dough ball gently with your fingers, and nestle one cashew half, if using, into each dough ball. Bake until the tops are lightly browned but the cookies are still slightly soft, 10 to 12 minutes. Cool on wire racks.

Poached Pears *French*

Moby Dick Hotel

Sandridge Road, Nahcotta, WA (360) 665-4543
www.mobydickhotel.com

At the hotel, Chef Jeff McMahon serves these beautifully colored pears with vanilla ice cream. They keep well, covered and refrigerated, for several days.

Serves 6

3	cups nonalcoholic red wine
1	cup granulated sugar
1	tablespoon grated nutmeg
1½	teaspoons ground allspice
1½	teaspoons ground cinnamon
1	teaspoon salt
6	pears, ripe, but not too soft

Preheat the oven to 350°F. In a medium saucepan, heat the red wine over low heat. Add the sugar, nutmeg, allspice, cinnamon and salt. Stir to dissolve the sugar and slowly bring to a boil. As the wine is heating, peel the pears and halve them lengthwise. Remove the stem, core and seeds.

Place the pears in a baking dish (they should fit snugly or the wine will not cover them). Pour the spiced wine over the top. Cover the dish with a close-fitting lid or with aluminum foil. Place the oven and bake for about 45 minutes. Remove and carefully (watch out for steam) check the pears for doneness. If a knife point enters easily, they are done. Allow to cool in the wine when done. Turn over any pears that are partially out of the wine and store overnight in the refrigerator. Reheat and serve.

Frank's Rice Pudding *American*

Keystone Café
395 W 5th Avenue, Eugene, OR (541) 342-2075

This recipe was developed by one of the bakers at the Keystone Cafe, Frank Cardozce. Some of the café's customers enjoy it for breakfast. Turbinado sugar is a pale brown sugar with coarse crystals. You may substitute a mixture of granulated and brown sugars if you like. Serve the pudding warm or cold.

Serves 8

1½	cups brown rice
3⅔	cups water
	Salt
2½	cups vanilla soymilk
⅔	cup turbinado sugar
1	(12-ounce) carton silken tofu

Place the rice, water and a pinch of salt in a medium saucepan and bring to a boil. Reduce heat to low, cover, and simmer until the rice is tender and the water has been absorbed, about 40 minutes. Remove from the heat and let the rice sit, covered for an additional 10 minutes.

Preheat the oven to 375°F. Have ready 8 ovenproof 1-cup capacity cups and a roasting pan large enough to hold them all. Place the soymilk, sugar, tofu, orange zest, vanilla and cinnamon in a blender and puree until smooth.

Divide the cooked brown rice evenly among the cups, placing about a heaping ½ cup in each. Add the blended ingredients to within ½ inch of the top. Top each pudding with a few raisins, if using, and freshly grated nutmeg.

Place the cups in the roasting pan and carefully pour enough hot tap water around them to come halfway up their sides. (You may find it easier to place the pan on the oven rack first and then pour the water into it). Bake the puddings until barely set, about 1 hour.

Fragrant Banana in Coconut Cream *Kuey Buod Chee, Thailand*

Chef Pranee Halvorsen
Presenter at Vegfest and chef at Monthly Dining Events
PCC Cooks Culinary instructor
www.Ilovethaicooking.com

"Kuey Buod Chee" means "a banana in a nun's hood" because the banana wears a robe of white coconut milk. This easy-to-make dessert can be served warm or cold from the refrigerator and is particularly nice with vanilla or coconut ice cream. It is also great to make a milk shake with any leftovers. It can be served with vanilla or coconut ice cream.

Serves 5

1½	cups water
1	cup coconut milk
½	cup granulated sugar
½	teaspoon salt
10	small ripe bananas, peeled and halved lengthwise
	Ground cinnamon

Place the water and ¼ cup of the coconut milk in a medium saucepan and bring to a boil. Reduce heat slightly, add the sugar and salt and simmer, stirring, until dissolved. Add the bananas and let the mixture simmer for one minute, then add the remaining coconut milk and cook to heat through. Serve the bananas with plenty of liquid so that the bananas will partially float. Sprinkle with cinnamon if desired.

Mango with Sweet Sticky Rice   Thailand

Thai Peppers Restaurant
222 N Lincoln Street, Port Angeles, WA (360) 452-4995

This is arguably the most popular dessert in Thailand; fortunately, if you have a steamer basket, it's easy to make. Sticky rice is sold in Asian markets and the international aisle of some supermarkets; look for rice that comes from Thailand or Laos. Palm sugar is a pale gold sugar sold in blocks at Asian markets. You may substitute light brown sugar.

Serves 4

- 2   cups sticky rice, soaked overnight in water to cover
- 1   cup coconut milk
- ½   cup palm sugar
      Pinch of salt
- 2   ripe mangoes
      Toasted sesame seeds or toasted coconut flakes (optional)

Drain the rice and steam it in a bamboo basket on full steam or high heat for 15 minutes. While the rice is cooking, combine the coconut milk, sugar and salt in a small saucepan and stir over low heat just until the sugar is dissolved. When the rice is done, pour the coconut milk mixture over the hot rice and stir to combine. Set aside.

Peel the mangoes and slice into thin slices. Place a scoop of sweet sticky rice on each plate and arrange some mango slices next to it. Sprinkle with toasted sesame seeds or toasted coconut flakes if desired.

Minted Green Grape Sorbet American

Chef Cheryl Redmond
Speaker at Vegfest
Food writer and editor
www.sredmond.com/vt_writing_svcs.htm

This refreshing sorbet tastes like frozen lemon-and-limeade. The amount of sugar can be adjusted to suit your taste and the sweetness of the grapes. The sorbet can be stored in the freezer for several days. If it becomes rock hard, you can soften it carefully in a microwave, provided that you stored it in a microwave safe container.

Serves 4

2 cups seedless green grapes	Grated zest of 1 orange, preferably organic
⅓ cup packed fresh mint leaves	
2 tablespoons fresh lime juice	1 teaspoon vanilla
4 tablespoons fresh lemon juice	1 teaspoon cinnamon
⅓–½ cup natural granulated sugar (like Sucanat)	Raisins (optional)
Pinch of salt	Freshly grated nutmeg

Put all the ingredients in the work bowl of a food processor and pulse several times to blend completely. Scrape down the sides of the bowl if necessary. Pour the mixture into a small metal bowl and place in the freezer. (Don't clean the food processor work bowl.) Freeze the mixture completely, about 3 hours.

Return the frozen mixture to the food processor and process until smooth and pale green in color. Serve immediately or refreeze in a covered container.

Lavender Sorbet *French*

The LocoMotive

291 E 5th Street, Eugene, OR (541) 465-4754
www.thelocomotive.com

This dessert is a must! It's both delicious and beautiful. Lavender grows exceptionally well in the Pacific Northwest, just as in Provence.

Serves 4

4¼   cups water
1¾   cups granulated sugar
   2   tablespoons plus 1 teaspoon fresh lavender blossoms (no stems)
   4   teaspoons freshly squeezed, strained lemon juice

Combine the water, sugar and lavender blossoms in a small saucepan. Bring the mixture to a boil; reduce the heat and simmer gently for 5 minutes. Remove from the heat and leave to steep for 5 more minutes. Add the lemon juice and stir thoroughly.

Pour the liquid through a fine-mesh strainer into a bowl, pressing hard on the blossoms to retrieve all of the juices.

Stir the liquid mixture well. Place it in an ice cream freezer and process according to the manufacturer's instructions.

About the Cookbook Team

AMANDA STROMBOM, *President of Vegetarians of Washington*

Amanda Strombom was inspired to become a vegetarian after reading the book *Fit for Life* by Harvey and Marilyn Diamond. She is originally from England, and came to Washington with her family in 1997 where her interest in vegetarianism continued to grow. In 2001, she joined Stewart Rose and two other friends who had just founded Vegetarians of Washington. As President of Vegetarians of Washington, she devotes many hours to helping people to improve their diet.

STEWART ROSE, *Vice President of Vegetarians of Washington*

Stewart Rose, an Orthodox Jew originally from New York, came to Washington in 1993 with his wife Susan. Stewart and Susan were inspired to become vegans many years ago while reading the Bible and continue to maintain their diet as part of their religious practice. Since its inception, Stewart has devoted much of his life to being Vice President of Vegetarians of Washington and to helping the organization grow so successfully. He currently resides in Bellevue, Washington with his wife and cat, Belle.

GRIGGS IRVING, *Managing Editor*

Griggs Irving began his adult life as an educator. At "mid-life" he left educational administration to enter the world of entrepreneurship. Among the myriad of positions in small, family or start-up businesses, was a stint in publishing. In the late '90s an impending health crisis and a meeting with Howard Lyman, author of *Mad Cowboy*, awakened him to the many values of a meat and dairy free diet. Griggs joined Vegetarians of Washington and became Managing Editor of the Veg-Feasting series.

CHERYL REDMOND, *Food Editor*

Cheryl Redmond is a freelance writer and editor who specializes in food and nutrition. She is the former associate food editor for *Natural Health* magazine and wrote the regular column "Natural Kitchen" as well as developing vegan recipes for the magazine. Cheryl also has a degree in pastry arts and has worked as a pastry chef for 10 years. Cheryl and her husband live in southern Vermont, where they recently finished building their house.

EDWINA CUSOLITO, *Graphic Designer*

For several years Edwina Cusolito has done freelance graphic design for Vegetarians of Washington. She recently designed the interior and cover for the successful guidebook, *Veg-Feasting in the Pacific Northwest.* There is synchronicity in her life and work. Not only is Edwina a committed vegetarian but her "day job" is staff graphic designer for PAWS, the Progressive Animal Welfare Society.

CASEY BLAKE, *Administrative Assistant*

Casey began her vegetarian life way back in college, after reading Frances Moore Lappe's *Diet for a Small Planet.* In the meantime, she has worked with small businesses as a technical writer. These combined life experiences have led her to be, among other things, former editor of Madison Market/Central Co-op's Natural Newsletter.

About Vegetarians of Washington

Vegetarians of Washington is an independent, nonprofit organization made up of people from all walks of life. We are the largest vegetarian organization in the Northwest, and one of the largest in the country. We are affiliated to the International Vegetarian Union, North American Vegetarian Society and are a member of the Provender Alliance.

You don't need to be a vegetarian to join! Many people join Vegetarians of Washington just to learn a little more about it all. We believe in providing a "can do" atmosphere where everybody proceeds at their own pace and just does the best they can.

At our gourmet monthly dining events, held at the Mount Baker Club in Seattle, you can enjoy a delicious multicourse meal from a different local restaurant, chef or cookbook author each month and meet lots of interesting people at one convenient location.

We also hold free informative nutrition and cooking classes at locations throughout western Washington, and fun social events such as hikes, picnics and Veggie Bowling. Our members receive a free subscription to the quarterly magazine, *Vegetarian Journal*, published by the nonprofit Vegetarian Resource Group. This unique magazine is packed full of recipes and the latest nutritional information. Our discount program entitles members to discounts from over 50 local restaurants and businesses.

This cookbook is the second book written by Vegetarians of Washington. The first was a guidebook to dining, shopping and living in Washington and Oregon, called *Veg-Feasting in the Pacific Northwest*. See page 239 for more information.

Our biggest event of the year is Vegfest, held in the Seattle Center in March each year. At this two day event, you can taste free food samples from almost 100 different companies, see cooking demonstrations by chefs from all over the country, hear the latest information on nutrition from our speakers and choose from a huge selection of vegetarian books. At the 2004 Vegfest, we gave out over 150,000 free samples of food.

The Vegetarians of Washington community education program includes presentations on the many benefits of a vegetarian diet to schools, colleges, churches, programs for disadvantaged mothers and children, hospitals, patient support groups, health clubs and community health fairs.

Many wonderful people have joined Vegetarians of Washington. We meet their needs by creating a positive atmosphere where they can socialize, have fun, eat great food together, and reinforce their excellent choice to follow a vegetarian diet. Please join us! For more information, please visit us on the Web at www.VegOfWA.org or call us at (206) 706-2635. To join, visit www.VegOfWA.org/joinus.html or copy the form on the back of this page, complete it and mail it in.

Membership Application

I /We would like to join Vegetarians of Washington.

Annual Fee *(Please check appropriate level)*
☐ $20-Individual   ☐ $35-Family   ☐ $50-Supporter   ☐ $100-Patron

Full Name(s) *For family memberships, please provide names of all family members who require a membership card.*

_____   _____

_____   _____

_____   _____

Address _____

City _____ State _____ Zip _____

Day Phone _____ Evening phone _____

Email: For family memberships, more than one email address can be provided if you wish. Please provide your email address so that we can send you newsflashes and reminders. We respect your privacy. Your contact details will not be shared with anyone, without your prior permission.

E-mail #1 _____

E-mail #2 _____

As part of your membership, you will automatically receive a free subscription to the quarterly publication, Vegetarian Journal, by mail unless you indicate otherwise.

Method of payment ☐ VISA   ☐ MasterCard   ☐ Check enclosed

Card number _____ Exp. date _____

Cardholder signature _____ Date _____

We are an independent 501(c)3 nonprofit organization. If your company offers matching gifts, please enclose the form with your payment.

Please make checks payable to:
Vegetarians of Washington
PO Box 85847
Seattle, WA 98145

Veg-Feasting
in the Pacific Northwest

This complete guide for vegetarians and the curious in Washington and Oregon includes:

- Over 300 Vegfriendly, Vegetarian and Vegan restaurants with reviews
- Over 120 Natural Food Stores with reviews
- Over 190 Farmers Markets
- 17 Articles by leading authorities on how and why to follow a vegetarian diet
- Below are a selection of quotes from the articles in this book.

In choosing a vegetarian diet as part of our strategy for healthy living, we can be confident that scientific evidence gives credence to our efforts.
   –Avoiding Cancer, F Patricia McEachrane Gross MD

A healthy vegetarian diet can meet the needs of both pregnant women and their infants.
   –Nutrition for Babies and Their Moms, Reed Mangels RD PhD FADA

Much of what we want for our children - healthy bodies with less illness, ability to concentrate, better study skills, adept physical ability, can be aided with a wholesome diet.
   –Attracting Your Child to Healthier Food, Cynthia Lair, Bastyr University

You're never too young to start watching your cholesterol because the process of clogged arteries begins in childhood.
   –Food for a Healthy Heart, Patricia McEachrane Gross MD

Vegetarians have just 1-2% of the national average of certain pesticides and industrial chemicals [in their bodies].
   –Beyond Fat and Cholesterol, Neal Barnard MD

A switch to a healthy vegetarian diet can help reverse many of the complications of diabetes even in advanced cases and can often prevent the disease from occurring in the first place.
   –Diet and Diabetes, Gregory Scribner MD

Bill Pearl, Mr. America and champion body builder, along with Edwin Moses, 400 meter gold medalist, are prime examples that muscular power and strength can be developed on vegetarian fuel.
—Winning the Race on a Vegetarian Diet, Scott Jurek MA PT

You will be surprised how easily change occurs when you take it one step at a time. Enjoy the journey along the way.
—Small Changes Make a Big Difference, Marilyn Joyce RD PhD

Studies have shown that populations that eat a diet high in vegetables and fruit and low in animal fat and meat…have a reduced risk of some of the more common cancers.
—Avoiding Cancer, Patricia McEachrane Gross MD

Experimental data proves the connection between high levels of animal protein in the diet and high osteoporosis rates.
—Nutrition for Healthy Bones, Ray Foster MD FACS

By providing yourself with food that helps diminish the effects of lower estrogen production in your body, you may help lessen the symptoms caused by less internally produced estrogen.
—Easing Menopause, Susan Gins MS CN

…eating more organic vegetarian foods, and keeping active both physically and mentally, all help ensure that our hearts and minds will remain healthy. These daily measures, so much less dramatic than drug effects, are nonetheless far more profound and effective. They are the keys to maintaining health into old age.
—Nutrition for Seniors, Heather Woods ND

Animal agriculture is unsustainable on a global scale. It produces food inefficiently and it consumes resources such as energy and water irresponsibly.
—The Environmental Case for Vegetarianism,
Anne I. Johnson BA and Timothy J. Fargo MA

Following a vegetarian diet has long been supported by many of the world's spiritual traditions. Dating back in some cases thousands of years, people of many different faiths have found a vegetarian diet to be an important part of their spiritual beliefs and practices. As time moves forward, more and more people are being inspired to adopt a vegetarian diet…Whatever religious or spiritual path you follow, a vegetarian diet is a perfect fit!
—Food and Faith, Stewart Rose BS Vice President Vegetarians of Washington

Saving the animals is easy… Enjoy the many delicious alternatives to meat, dairy and eggs, and you'll be saving the animals with every bite.
    –Saving the Animals with every bite, Jennifer Hillman MA

Although you use them in small amounts, herbs and spices make a big contribution to your meals.
    –The Well Stocked Kitchen, Cheryl Redmond, Food Editor

As more people discover the many benefits of a vegetarian diet, there has been a steady increase in the number of vegetarian restaurants throughout the Pacific Northwest. There is also a growing trend for general restaurants to offer more vegetarian options.
    –Dining Out, Stewart Rose, Vice President, Vegetarians of Washington

Start by getting to know your local food co-op, natural food store, super market natural food section or farmer's market. Take a stroll down the aisles and see how many of the products are familiar to you. Keep an eye out for new varieties and flavors of old favorites.
    –Shopping For the Vegetarian Kitchen,
    Stewart Rose, Vice President, Vegetarians of Washington

The first step in creating a healthy meal is to make sure that you have wholesome ingredients on hand.
    –The Well Stocked Kitchen, Cheryl Redmond, Food Editor

At Vegetarians of Washington, we ask only that you are willing to experiment and willing to learn, and that you do the best you can.
    –Cookbooks and Other Helpful Resources,
    Amanda Strombom MA, President, Vegetarians of Washington

Many people rave about how useful this book has been to them, whether they live in Washington or Oregon, or are just visiting. Vegetarian Journal says of our guidebook, *"With Vegetarians of Washington's help, eating vegetarian in the Northwest now couldn't be any easier."*

Veg-Feasting in the Pacific Northwest, published by the Book Publishing Company, is available at bookstores, natural food stores and online. Please visit www.vegofwa.org to learn more about this book.

Other Resources

The Vegetarian Resource Group
The Vegetarian Resource Group is a national nonprofit organization, which makes it easier to be vegetarian. Its registered dietitians, educators and activists assist consumers, businesses, health professionals and food services. Their public policy work is creating new opportunities for future generations of vegetarians. They are publishers of many books including *Simply Vegan, Meatless Meals for Working People, Vegetarian Journal's Guide to Natural Foods Restaurants in the U.S. and Canada, Vegan Diabetes Meal Plan, Vegan Passover Recipes, Vegetarian Journal,* and more. Their website, www.vrg.org is the most popular vegetarian website.
The Vegetarian Resource Group
P.O. Box 1463, Baltimore, Maryland 21203; (410) 366-8343 (VEGE); vrg@vrg.org; www.vrg.org

Northwest VEG
For information on vegetarian events and happenings in Oregon, please visit www.nwveg.org or call (503) 224-7380.

Index